MW00654431

JAMES,
YOUR BROTHER

By LEHMAN STRAUSS

The First Person
The Second Person
The Third Person

Prophetic Mysteries Revealed
The Prophecies of Daniel
Devotional Studies in Galatians and Ephesians
Devotional Studies in Philippians
James Your Brother
The Epistles of John
The Book of the Revelation

Certainties for Today
The Eleven Commandments
We Live Forever

Demons, Yes—but Thank God for Good Angels

JAMES, YOUR BROTHER

Studies in the Epistle of James

BY

LEHMAN STRAUSS

✿✿

LOIZEAUX BROTHERS
Neptune, New Jersey

FIRST EDITION, OCTOBER 1956
THIRTEENTH PRINTING, DECEMBER 1989

COPYRIGHT 1956, BY LEHMAN STRAUSS

ISBN 0-87213-818-6
PRINTED IN THE UNITED STATES OF AMERICA

PREFATORY NOTE

Some of life's most cherished treasures have lain unused, hence unappreciated. The writer believes now that he had too long neglected the worthful words that the Apostle James in his epistle gave us by the Holy Spirit. It is with deep regret that the writer's life and ministry have been deprived of so precious a portion of God's truth as was left to us by the brother of our Lord.

If the reader of these studies receives but a small part of the blessing that came in writing them, the author will be repaid for his efforts.

The writer hereby expresses his deepest gratitude to Mrs. Marion Beal, Mrs. Martha Benesol, Miss Helen Hertzler, and Mrs. Ellen Thornton for ably assisting in preparing the manuscript for publication.

Lehman Strauss

Bristol, Pennsylvania
1956

CONTENTS

How I praise Thee, precious Saviour,
That Thy love laid hold of me;
Thou hast saved and cleansed and filled me
That I might Thy channel be.

Emptied that Thou shouldest fill me,
A clean vessel in Thy hand;
With no power but as Thou givest
Graciously with each command.

Witnessing Thy power to save me,
Setting free from self and sin;
Thou who boughtest to possess me,
In Thy fullness, Lord, come in.

Jesus, fill now with Thy Spirit
Hearts that full surrender know;
That the streams of living water
From our inner man may flow.

Channels only, blessed Master,
But with all Thy wondrous pow'r
Flowing thro' us, Thou canst use us
Every day and every hour.

INTRODUCTION TO
THE EPISTLE OF JAMES

James 1:1
1. James, a servant of God and of the Lord Jesus Christ, to the twelve tribes which are scattered abroad, greeting.

These devotional studies in the Epistle of James are the result of a twofold desire in the writer's heart. First, I have been looking forward for some time to a closer study of this little book for personal spiritual profit and growth in grace. As a minister of God's Word, I always anticipate passing on to others those lessons learned. Secondly, for some time I have had a growing conviction that this epistle has been greatly neglected. Now if these studies will make any contribution whatever to the spiritual growth of some, or if they will awaken in others an interest in a portion of God's Word that has passed into near-oblivion, I shall consider my effort worthwhile.

Although we praise God for the contributions that have been made to the world through men like Martin Luther, it is to be regretted that his influence upon many has not always been for good. In terming the Book of James "a veritable epistle of straw, and destitute of evangelic character," he is responsible for turning many away from this portion. But the Epistle of James is not an epistle of straw; rather is it an epistle of strength. It is not destitute of evangelic character but rather characteristic of the evangel.

The idea promulgated by Luther that James and Paul are contradictory on the matter of justification is erroneous also. Although Paul wrote that "a man is justified by faith" (Rom. 3:28) and James wrote "Ye see then how that by works a man is justified, and not by faith only" (James 2:24), close exami-

3

nation will reveal that rather than being contradictory, each is complementary to the other.

Paul deals with the inner faith of man's heart as God sees it, while James concerns his discourse with the outward fruits of faith as man sees them. God knows whether or not I am a true believer on the basis of my faith apart from any works, but men can only know whether or not I am a true believer as they observe my life outwardly. Jesus said *we* can distinguish between the true and the false only by a man's fruits (Matt. 7:16, 21).

The theme of this epistle throughout is an extremely practical one, dealing with truth applied and heavenly wisdom resulting in a holy walk. James sounds the much needed and much neglected note which demands conduct conformable to creed, behavior commensurate with belief, and deportment compatible with doctrine. In substance James is appealing for reality in religion.

The rejection of any portion of the Holy Scriptures is dangerous, but it is doubly so when the passages rejected deal with practical holiness before men. The world needs to see a demonstration of God's love and power in Christ's true Church. Satan does all in his power to subdue, and even destroy, such a witness. James, by the Holy Spirit, appeals to every believer to walk holily before God and man. Luther thought he saw a conflict between James and Paul, and in his human reasoning he did the dangerous thing when he rejected James.

The Epistle is the first of seven general or catholic Epistles. The term "catholic" is applied to certain Epistles of the New Testament addressed to groups of churches or Christians in general. The Catholic Epistles are James, First and Second Peter, First, Second, and Third John, and Jude. Two of these authors are Apostles, Peter and John; and two of them are brothers of Jesus. If it were written between 45 and 55 A.D., it would be one of the earliest if not the first book of the New Testament to be written.

The writer of this Epistle, as do Paul, Peter, and Jude, identifies himself immediately as to his name and position, and includes those to whom he addresses himself.

The human author of this epistle is not easily distinguished from several other New Testament men of the same name. The Scriptures speak of not less than six persons called *James*. These are: (1) the son of Zebedee (Mark 1:19); (2) the son of Alphaeus (Mark 3:18); (3) "James the less" (Mark 15:40); (4) one referred to as one of Jesus' brothers (Mark 6:3); (5) "James the Lord's brother" (Gal. 1:19); and (6) the brother of Jude (Jude 1). Upon checking the above Scriptures, one can clearly see that these six can actually be reduced to three if we regard two and three as the same person, and four, five, and six as the same person. Three men called *James* remain: James, the son of Zebedee; James, the son of Alphaeus; and James, the Lord's brother.

Now the question arises as to which of the three wrote the epistle. James the son of Zebedee, the brother of John, could not be the author since he was killed with the sword by Herod before the Epistle was written (Acts 12:2). Some claim that James the son of Alphaeus wrote the Epistle. But how then could he be called the brother of our Lord? The Roman Catholic Church would be inclined to favor James the son of Alphaeus since it would support their invention of the perpetual virginity of Mary. This writer believes that children were born to Joseph and Mary after the birth of our Lord Jesus Christ. In Luke 2:7 our Lord is spoken of as Mary's first-born son, implying that others might have been born later. Also, the account in Matthew suggests that Joseph and Mary entered into natural marriage relations after the birth of our Lord (Matt. 1:18, 25). We believe that the author of our Epistle was a brother to our Lord, born of Joseph and Mary after the birth of Jesus Christ.

Although James was reared in the same home with the Lord Jesus, James apparently did not become a believer until after Jesus arose from death and the grave. Even after our Lord began His public ministry, John wrote: "For neither did His brethren

believe in Him" (John 7:5). Again Paul indicated in his letter
to the Corinthians: "He rose again the third day . . . After that,
He was seen of James; then of all the apostles" (1 Cor. 15:4, 7).

Most important of all, however, is the fact that James, the
brother of Jesus Christ, did come to believe that Jesus was the
Son of God; he did appropriate Christ's Gospel; he did grow in
grace, even the knowledge of his Lord and Saviour Jesus Christ;
and he later was recognized as a leader in the Church at Jerusalem. James indeed spoke with authority and spiritual discernment at the Church Council, and that to the pleasure and satisfaction of the apostles and elders (Acts 15:13-22).

"A servant of God and of the Lord Jesus Christ." Like Paul
(Rom. 1:1; Titus 1:1) and Peter (2 Peter 1:1), James refers to
himself, not as an apostle, but as a bondslave. The word "servant" denotes this. Any truly great man of God, regardless of how
high his position in the church, regards himself as a servant of
Christ.

The step from darkness to light is a transfer from slavery to
Satan and sin to bond-slavery to Jesus Christ. In the redemptive
process the enslaved victim is purchased by Jesus Christ from
the slave market of sin to become the possession of the Purchaser. "Ye are not your own? For ye are bought with a price"
(1 Cor. 6:19, 20). "Ye are bought with a price; be not ye the
servants of men" (1 Cor. 7:23). Our redemption included deliverance from the bitter bondage of sin into the blessed bondage of the Saviour.

Since the Son has made us free from Satan we are free indeed
(John 8:36) to serve our Saviour. Peter describes this as the position of every true believer when he writes: "As free, and not
using your liberty for a cloke of maliciousness, but as the servants of God" (1 Peter 2:16).

J. Nieboer tells the following story to illustrate the attitude of
a willing slave. The incident took place at a slave auction in the
Southland during the days of slavery. A fine-looking young man
was placed on the block for sale. Among the interested bidders

was an Englishman who outbid a number of other interested buyers. When the deal was finally consummated, the young slave chided his purchaser for buying a slave when slavery was already abolished in England. To the young man's chiding the purchaser replied: "I have bought you to set you free." Overcome with emotion, the slave said: "Sir, I will be your willing slave forever."

Oh, my dear Christian friend, now that Christ has set us free from sin's bondage, who among us would not gladly be His bond-slave forever? Let us recognize anew our position as servants "of the Lord Jesus Christ" and rejoice in this blessed servitude!

A servant of God must of necessity be a servant of the Lord Jesus Christ. As Christ's true servant James testifies to the deity of the Son of God (1:1; 2:1). He sees the Father and the Son co-equal with each other. The self-styled "Jehovah's Witnesses" who deny the deity of our Lord Jesus Christ are in reality the emissaries of Satan. Our Lord said: "All men should honour the Son, even as they honour the Father. He that honoureth not the Son honoureth not the Father which hath sent Him" (John 5:23). Later He added: "If God were your Father, ye would love Me" (John 8:42). and "He that hateth Me hateth My Father also" (John 15:23). John by the Holy Spirit writes: "Whosoever denieth the Son, the same hath not the Father" (1 John 2:23). Let us never fail to acknowledge the Lordship of Mary's Son who is in reality the anointed Son of God. The measure of our love for Him determines the measure of our love for the Father who sent him.

The epistle was written in the primary sense "to the twelve tribes which are scattered abroad." At the time of writing it would seem that James had a special burden for the dispersed Jews. There were many Jewish Christians who were scattered through persecution.

In comparison to the often-used phrase "the ten lost tribes," this reference to "the twelve tribes" holds special interest, some having gone so far as to attempt to identify the "ten lost tribes"

as the British people. As for this writer, the theory of British
Israelism has been satisfactorily disproved. Moreover, the Bible
speaks nowhere of "the lost tribes." While a man's identity may
not be known to himself, it is still known fully to God. When our
Lord returns to earth again, the twelve different tribes shall once
more be known to all. He shall bring them together (Rev. 7:4-8).

The scattering of the Jews was not only known to God but predicted by God from the beginning. God had told His people: "I
will scatter you among the nations" (Lev. 26:33). This scattering commenced when the ten tribes were carried away into
Assyrian captivity about 740 B.C. and it has continued down
through the centuries. It is generally conceded that the infiltra-
tion of Jews in every country has added to the advancement of
civilization throughout the known world. God has used the scattering for the good of humanity.

This principle of scattering helped spread the Gospel in the
early Church. Luke reminds us that "at that time there was a
great persecution against the church which was at Jerusalem; and
they were scattered abroad throughout the regions of Judaea
and Samaria" (Acts 8:1). "Therefore they that were scattered
abroad went every where preaching the Word" (Act 8:4). When
God permitted the scattering of His children at that time it was
for the purpose of reaching the unreached with the gospel of
Jesus Christ. Certainly we cannot think for a moment that God
had forsaken them nor that He had lost track of them. No,
never! He knew each one by name as well as the whereabouts of
each, just as He possesses full knowledge of each child of His today. At the Rapture of the Church He will gather the redeemed
of the Church Age unto Himself even as He will gather the
twelve tribes when Christ returns to earth.

The heart passion of James for the Jewish Christians all over
the world should be ours for the whole Body of Jesus Christ, His
Church, on earth, whether visible or invisible.

O peace divine and pure,
In wildest storm secure,
That feels the summer's glow
'Mid wintry ice and snow;
When may I rise to this dear prize,
And fill my breast with inward rest?

My life is tempest-tossed,
With wayward currents crossed,
Unhallowed cares deface
The soul's most holy place;
How may I bind these cares, and find
All passion spent in calm content?

And though through storm and stress
I sail the vasty seas
Of troubled thought—in vain
I toil the shore to gain:
For yet within I'd feel my sin,
And still afar would shine Thy star.

Lord, only from Thy face
Beams forth this mystic grace,
And only in Thy love,
Beneath, around, above,
May my weak soul grow great and whole,
And peace divine be fully mine.

PATIENCE THROUGH
TRIBULATION

James 1:2-4

2. My brethren, count it all joy when ye fall into divers temptations;

3. Knowing this, that the trying of your faith worketh patience.

4. But let patience have her perfect work, that ye may be perfect and entire, wanting nothing.

We proceed now to the very heart of the Epistle.

This first major lesson with which James deals: namely, *Patience Through Tribulation,* is a paradox to every unregenerated man, and even strange to the Christian not well taught in the Word. It is to Christians that James addresses this message, calling them "My brethren." The term is used here not in a national sense but in a spiritual one. All true believers in the Lord Jesus Christ have God as their Father and are therefore brethren. Obviously it is one of the favorite expressions of James, for he uses it not less than seventeen times (1:2, 9, 16, 19, 2:1, 5, 14, 15; 3:1, 10, 12; 4:11; 5:7, 9, 10, 12, 19).

To his persecuted and dispersed brethren in Christ, the author writes: "Count it all joy when ye fall into divers temptations." The word "temptations" here means "trials" or "tests" with no thought whatever of solicitation to do wrong. James teaches us that tribulation is one of the tests of faith. Our Lord spoke of His trials (Luke 22:28), as did also Paul (Acts 20:18, 19). Peter likewise wrote of "heaviness through manifold temptations [or testings]" (1 Peter 1:6). The believer's trials are said, then, to be "divers" (varied) and manifold (many).

That a child of God should have to pass through many and various trials has been difficult for some Christians to accept. In my experiences as a pastor I receive not a few inquiries on this very problem. Possibly some people have misunderstood, feeling that the Christian is expected to count pain and sorrow as good things in themselves and therefore a source of joy. I do not believe this to be the meaning in the statement James makes. Elsewhere in Scripture we are told that "no chastening for the *present* seemeth to be joyous, but grievous . . ." (Heb. 12:11). But then we are not living merely for the "present." For each of us there is the *"afterward,"* the future prospect, and "it yieldeth the peaceable fruit of righteousness unto them which are exercised thereby."

Who among us would not be glad if the fruits of affliction could be produced by some experience of a more pleasant nature? But not one of us has any right to question God's methods in producing His desired fruits. He knows that the bitter agonies of sorrow and suffering are needed to conquer sin. It was through the agony of His own soul and the shame and suffering of His Holy Son that the sin question was satisfactorily dealt with at Calvary.

Herein lies the victory: it is possible to rejoice *in* the trial. Of our Lord Jesus Christ it is written, "Who for the *joy* that was set before Him endured the cross, despising the shame . . ." (Heb. 12:2). This was the experience of many in the early church. Peter and the other Apostles turned from their persecutors *"rejoicing* that they were counted worthy to suffer shame for His name" (Acts 5:41). It is possible for one to obey this Spirit-directed admonition of James.

Although it may be an unusual perspective, it is true nevertheless that nothing but divine love sends trouble to the child of God, "For whom the Lord loveth He chasteneth, and scourgeth every son whom He receiveth" (Heb. 12:6). When, in the first shocking moment, I look my trouble in the face, it is hard for me to recognize any blessing in it. Usually I count it all joy when I escape trials and tribulations. How do you react to trouble? Do you ever think of a heavy burden or affliction someone carries, and then thank God that you have been delivered? Of such an experience, Charles Brown says: "It is just possible—according to James—that they are to be envied and we to be pitied." James appeals to us to recognize that every test, every trial, every tribulation, with all the accompanying sorrow and disappointment, is a God-given opportunity for growth and development in the Christian life.

My brother in Christ, Richard H. Seume, inserted the following clipping in his "Studies in James." I beg his patience with me as I quote it here. It is entitled: "The Blessing of Irritations."

"Life on earth would not be worth much if every source of irritation were removed. Yet most of us rebel against the things that irritate us, and count as heavy loss what ought to be rich gain. We are told that the oyster is wiser; that when an irritating object, like a bit of sand, gets under the 'mantle' of his shell, he simply covers it with the most precious part of his being and makes of it a pearl. The irritation that it was causing is stopped by encrusting it with the pearly formation. A true pearl is therefore simply a VICTORY over irritation. Every irritation that gets into our lives today is an opportunity for pearl culture. The more irritations the devil flings at us, the more pearls we may have. We need only to welcome them and cover them completely with love, that most precious part of us, and the irritation will be smothered out as the pearl comes into being. What a store of pearls we may have, if we will!"

Trials are not a sign of God's displeasure, for the Apostle Peter tells us that we are not to think it strange when some trial comes to test us as though some strange thing happened to us (1 Peter 4:12). The Lord Jesus said: "In the world ye shall have tribulation" (John 16:33). Beloved, if we know these things we will not be caught unguarded when trials come.

Remember, *all things,* even our sorest troubles, work together for good to them that love God (Romans 8:28). Failing to reckon upon this and becoming disconsolate and discouraged under trial brings no glory to God. Moreover, a grumbler places his own limits on his usefulness in the service of the Lord. Joy is contagious, and joy under fire brings blessing to others.

The world will not understand our joy in the midst of tribulation, but they certainly should see it. Poor Elijah! When he fled from Jezebel, sat under the juniper tree, and requested to die, he had no testimony before God or man (1 Kings 19:4). On the other hand, when Paul and Silas were chained in prison they counted it all joy even though their backs bled from the beatings and their feet were held fast in stocks. They sang praises and prayed to God, and in the midst of rejoicing in tribulation they led an entire family to Jesus Christ (Acts 16:23-33). After such an experience Paul could say to others: "Rejoice in the Lord alway: and again I say, Rejoice" (Phil. 4:4).

In *verse three* James continues with a reason why the believer is to count it all joy when adversities come to him. The reason? "Knowing this, that the trying of your faith *worketh* patience." Ah, the test of faith then is something that *works*. It produces something, and that something is the much needed patience which is obviously lacking in most of us. Keep in mind the fact that James, throughout his Epistle, is pleading for a belief that behaves, a faith that is followed by fruit. Now the presence of patience in one who is being tested is no proof that such a one is saved; but, contrariwise, where there is a living faith in the Lord Jesus Christ, patience should be manifest at all times. Where patience is lacking in one of His children, God has a working remedy—"the trying of your faith."

Rejoice, not because trials come, but because of their possible benefits. James says that our trials may produce *patience* in this life; Peter adds that trials produce *praise* at the appearing of Jesus Christ (1 Peter 1:7). Patience before men, and praise before God—what a blessed combination! But beware lest the trial of our faith should work impatience, for then a beautiful thing is lost in this life and there shall be no praise of our Lord in the life to come. Where faith is genuine, tribulation will only increase one's perseverance, for "tribulation worketh patience" (Romans

5:3). A trial is not something to be tolerated but a trust to be treasured.

Patience is a virtue that aids in developing Christian character. In a true sense it is the quietness or self-possession of one's own spirit in resignation to God's will. But this is only one aspect of its meaning. Patience is also positive and aggressive; it sees a divinely set goal and with determined perseverance pursues it. Paul expressed this positive aspect of it when he testified: "I press toward the mark for the prize of the high calling of God in Christ Jesus" (Phil. 3:14). Paul's will was submissive to God's will whenever the Apostle was called to suffer and in this he displayed a passive patience; but his life was marked also by a progressive, persevering patience, and the latter was developed by the former. Tribulation led Paul to trust more and try harder. It settled him into sweet acquiescence on the one hand and stirred him to stiffer action on the other. In every trial God is working to perfect patience.

G. Coleman Luck, in his fine little book (#251. Moody Colportage Library), tells how a young minister, realizing he lacked patience, once asked an older man of God to pray that he might have more patience. The aged man knelt beside his younger brother in the Lord and began to pray that God would send trouble and difficulties upon the youth. After a while the younger brother tapped the older minister upon the shoulder and whispered: "You must have misunderstood me; I asked that you would pray that I might have more patience, not more trouble." Then the older man replied: "The Scripture says: 'Tribulation worketh patience.' That is the only way!"

Since all the foregoing is true: namely, that our heavenly Father uses tribulation in the lives of His children in order to produce patience, and it is likewise true that we "have need of patience" (Heb. 10:36), the next word from James demands our careful attention. He adds: "But let patience have her perfect work, that ye may be perfect and entire, wanting nothing" (verse 4). Williams translates this verse to read: "But you must let your endurance come to its perfect product, so that you may be fully developed and perfectly equipped." Do not give up but persevere until you are certain that God has perfected in you that virtue which needs His cultivation. God wants each of us who is His child to be full grown, mature, lacking in no spiritual thing.

Have you a desire to grow up into Jesus Christ? Does your heart yearn to be conformed to His image? In order for this to be accomplished in your life God asks for complete surrender to His will.

God's goal for us, completeness with nothing lacking, is expressed in the word "perfect" and the Holy Spirit will use every trial accepted in the right Scriptural sense to produce in us a maturity of Christian character.

"Rest in the Lord, and wait patiently for Him" (Psalm 37:7). Sooner or later your trial will come to an end; and remember, "There hath no temptation taken you but such as is common to man: but God is faithful, who will not suffer you to be tempted above that ye are able; but will with the temptation also make a way to escape, that ye may be able to bear it" (1 Cor. 10:13).

Before ending this meditation on *Patience Through Tribulation,* I am led to comment on *verse twelve* since it is a necessary part of our theme. "Blessed is the man that endureth temptation: for when he is tried, he shall receive the crown of life, which the Lord hath promised to them that love Him" (1:12). The word "temptation" in this verse means the same as in verse two, not a solicitation to do wrong as in verse thirteen, but *"trial"* or *"testing."* Verse twelve sums up the matter of patient endurance under trial in that it promises a reward for all who endure trial. That reward is *"the crown of life."* Although God will reward the faithful pastor, soul winner, teacher, and evangelist, He has a special reward ready for the patient sufferer. I am sure that this crown will be given to some whose names are not known beyond the bounds of their own circle of family and friends, possibly some blind, some paralyzed, some shut-in with an incurable disease, some husband or wife who endured the trials brought on by the persecution of an unbelieving mate, yes, and a host of others whose trials are not known to any but God and themselves.

Do we love Him, our blessed Lord and Saviour Jesus Christ? If we do, we will endure every trial for His sake, and when He comes for us He will bring the reward with him—"the crown of life."

(For a study on the other crowns mentioned in the Bible, see the author's book, *We Live Forever*.)

I could not do without Thee,
   O Saviour of the lost,
Whose precious blood redeemed me
   At such tremendous cost:
Thy righteousness, Thy pardon,
   Thy Sacrifice, must be
My only hope and comfort,
   My glory and my plea.

I could not do without Thee,
   I cannot stand alone,
I have no strength or goodness,
   No wisdom of my own:
But Thou, beloved Saviour,
   Art all in all to me;
And weakness will be power,
   If leaning hard on Thee.

I could not do without Thee,
   For years are fleeting fast,
And soon in solemn silence
   The river must be passed:
But Thou wilt never leave me;
   And, though the waves run high,
I know Thou wilt be near me,
   And whisper, "It is I."

WISDOM THROUGH
PRAYER

James 1:5-8

5. If any of you lack wisdom, let him ask of God, that giveth to all men liberally, and upbraideth not; and it shall be given him.

6. But let him ask in faith, nothing wavering. For he that wavereth is like a wave of the sea driven with the wind and tossed.

7. For let not that man think that he shall receive any thing of the Lord.

8. A double minded man is unstable in all his ways.

James now takes up the subject matter of his second lesson: namely, *wisdom*. In the first lesson (verses 2-4) we learned that patience is obtained through trial. In this second lesson (verses 5-8) we are to learn that wisdom is obtained through prayer. The second lesson is closely related to the first since there is no greater need for wisdom than when one is passing through some deep trial of affliction. It is difficult to act wisely when we have been wronged or when we are suffering.

Wisdom is discernment and judgment and dexterity in the application of knowledge already gained, not only in the arts and sciences but also in the Scriptures. One may have acquired vast knowledge but lack wisdom. Wisdom does not concern itself with theories and ideas but with suiting the right means to the right end. Knowledge becomes baggage when we lack the faculty of using it to attain perfect and right goals. Wisdom does the right thing in the right way and is certainly one of the most needed but grandest of virtues.

The outstanding characteristic of this generation is the absence of true wisdom. This may offend the more highly educated. We have never had more college graduates and never more educated ignorance. Through knowledge man has learned to travel faster than sound but shows his lack of wisdom by going faster in the wrong direction. Through knowledge we have accumulated piles of information about the world we live in, but show our lack of wisdom by not learning any better how to live in the world.

It is a bad thing when a man lacks wisdom, but it is far worse when that man is so wise in his own conceit that he rejects the true wisdom which comes from God. Some men are born with an alacrity to grasp knowledge, but when that knowledge is set against God and His Word, those men become dangerous.

James says: "If any [man] of you lack wisdom, let him ask of God."

We Christians cannot afford to make decisions on our own. God knows what is best for His children, and we need to come humbly requesting wisdom for every issue of life. After all, God's will is best for us.

When we need understanding we must ask God to enlighten us. A multitude of situations arise in which we become conscious that we "lack wisdom." Our brethren in Christ may offer us good advice, but before we go to them we should "ask of God." Solomon asked, praying: "O Lord my God . . . Give . . . Thy servant an understanding heart to judge Thy people, that I may discern between good and bad . . . And God said unto him . . . Behold, I have done according to thy words: lo, I have given thee a wise and an understanding heart" (1 Kings 3:7-12). What God did for Solomon He will do for any of His children. Let a Christian ask God for wisdom to do the right thing and not the wrong, and he can be certain of that prayer being answered.

Doubtless many believers among us desire the wisdom of God but do not know how to go about getting it. There is a proverb which says: "Wisdom is the principal thing; therefore get wisdom: and with all thy getting get understanding" (Prov. 4:7). The Bible tells us what things we are to seek after and how we are to go about getting them. In the matter of wisdom it is given to those of God's children who ask for it. James says: "If any of you lack wisdom, let him ask of God." Here is a simple definition of prayer: a definite request for something which we lack, and that something is wisdom.

Look with me at a significant verse from one of the Psalms. The Psalmist writes: "The fear of the Lord is the beginning of wisdom" (Psalm 111:10). If we want to understand the will of God, it is of the utmost importance that we be right with God Himself. The person who has no respect nor reverence for God is anything but wise. This verse shows us the test of common sense.

Wisdom, no matter how high or perfect, has its roots in submissiveness to the laws of God. Only a fool denies or defies God. A Plato, an Aristotle, a Socrates, a Tacitus may accumulate vast knowledge and seek to know wisdom, but until the philosopher bows in humble reverence before the sovereign God, he knows not anything. An Einstein may be a genius in mathematics, but without God in his life he must go on the records as a man without wisdom. And permit me here to tell you that he was exactly just that. At a conference attended by outstanding churchmen and scientists, a paper was read from Albert Einstein in which he said: "In their struggle for the ethical good, teachers of religion must have the stature to give up the doctrine of a personal god." Let the Word of God answer the like of Einstein: "The fool hath said in his heart, There is no God" (Psalm 14:1).

Job raised the question, "But where shall wisdom be found? and where is the place of understanding?" (Job 28:12). The remainder of the chapter answers this universal question. Wisdom is not found in the land of the living (verse 13) nor in the depth of the sea (verse 14); it cannot be purchased with the gold of Ophir (verses 15, 16) nor with the precious stones of the earth, "for the price of wisdom is above rubies" (verses 17-19). Then God answered the quest of His child, "And unto man He said, Behold, the fear of the Lord, that is wisdom; and to depart from evil is understanding" (verse 28).

God is the Author and the source of all wisdom. He planned

the universe and man. He alone knows the intricate workings of all things, and His wisdom He gives only to those who fear Him. A man may look deeply into science and philosophy for true wisdom, but he will look in vain. Joseph was a prisoner in Egypt, yet because he feared God he was possessed of a wisdom greater by far than that of the wise men and astrologers of Egypt. Daniel was a captive in Babylon, yet he could advise the king and Babylon's wisest of worldly-wise men, because he feared God. Paul was a prisoner in chains, yet he could advise the navigators on the sea better than they knew themselves, because he feared God. Most certainly the fear of the Lord is the beginning of wisdom. Shut out God from your life and you list yourself among the fools.

Look now at the process by which God imparts His perfect wisdom to man. We would miss a great deal in our study on wisdom if we failed to look at a New Testament classic which contrasts worldly wisdom with divine wisdom. I am thinking of Paul's record in 1 Corinthians 1:18-31, where God says: "I will destroy the wisdom of the wise, and will bring to nothing the understanding of the prudent" (verse 19).

Whenever a man like Einstein chooses to stand with the philosophical thought that denies God, he places himself on the side that cannot win. If men like Einstein had pure and perfect wisdom, why did not God choose such men as His servants and messengers? Verse 20 asks: "Where is the wise [the thinker]? where is the scribe [the writer]? where is the disputer [the speaker]?" Not one man, regardless of how able a thinker, writer, or speaker he might be, has ever been called of God to speak or write for Him if he did not reverently fear God. God completely bypasses the worldly-wise man who denies Him, since, by divine decrees, the world through its own wisdom cannot know God (verse 21). God rejects the wisdom of this world and employs the foolishness of preaching to save men "Because the foolishness of God [in man's estimate] is wiser than men; and the weakness of God [in man's estimate] is stronger than men" (verse 25).

Now in verse 30 we come to the contrast between the wise and the strong in human sight and the wise and strong in God's sight. "But of him are ye in Christ Jesus, who of God is made unto us wisdom, and righteousness, and sanctification, and redemption" (verse 30). Since Christ is God manifest in the flesh, He is the perfect expression of the divine attribute of wisdom, and the moment a man exercises saving faith in Jesus Christ he is in touch with true wisdom.

The divinely appointed starting place, then, is the believing sinner's contact with the Lord of Wisdom at this meeting place. Things which, without Him, are impossible to procure are made available through Christ. One of these is wisdom. The Christian does not obtain his wisdom from men like Plato, Aristotle, Socrates, Einstein, or some other philosopher or scientist of renown, but from the Lord Jesus Christ. Thus Christ is made unto every believer "wisdom." Even as the origin of our union with Christ is of God, so in its effect, Christ is made unto us all that God is. Here its effect is stated as wisdom. Union with the Lord Jesus Christ makes the believer truly wise.

Most men whom God has used have been men from the common walks of life, men who believed in Jesus Christ and were empowered by the Holy Spirit to do great works for Him. Occasionally God saved and used someone who would have made his mark among the people of his day, but such were in the minority. Paul was one of them. He later wrote: *"Not many wise men after the flesh, not many mighty, not many noble, are called"* (verse 26). But God is choosing and using humble men to whom He can speak and impart divine wisdom for every emergency in this life. By relegating the wisdom of men to its insignificant place, God elevates to its rightful high position a simple trust in His Son.

Moreover, God giveth "liberally." God's liberality is seen on every hand. We have more of most things than we actually need. I know a dear saint of God who enjoys a measure of health and happiness, yet she has had seven major operations which necessitated the removal of one lung, one kidney, one breast, a part of the intestine, and the appendix.

God is equally liberal in giving spiritual gifts to those who ask. If you ask for wisdom in order that you may do right, you can expect God to give liberally of His wisdom.

And you may rest assured He will not upbraid you. He "upbraideth not." Men may scold us when we ask of them, but God, never. You will never hear God say to you, "You made your bed, so lie in it." A little lad of ten years asked his father twice in one evening for information concerning a problem in arithmetic. The father, a bit annoyed, replied: "Use your own common sense and figure it out for yourself." Our heavenly Father never upbraids his children in such fashion. He giveth freely. "He that spared not His own Son, but delivered Him up for us all, how shall He not with Him also freely give us all things?"

Possibly at some time in your life you have asked direction but did not feel that God actually gave you that wisdom for which you sought. James deals in part with this problem of unanswered prayer. He adds: "But let him ask in faith, nothing wavering. For he that wavereth is like a wave of the sea driven with the wind and tossed. For let not that man think that he shall receive any thing of the Lord" (verses 6, 7).

What earthly parent does not want the confidence and faith of his children? Just as any mother and father would be displeased should the children show lack of faith in them, so "without faith it is impossible to please Him [God]" (Heb. 11:6). God has decreed that faith is an essential requisite to answered prayer. "All things, whatsoever ye shall ask in prayer, believing, ye shall receive" (Matt. 21:22). "What things soever ye desire, when ye pray, believe that ye receive them, and ye shall have them" (Mark 11:24).

While God will not upbraid His children for asking, we have one instance on record where our risen Lord met with His disciples "and upbraided them with their unbelief and hardness of heart, because they believed not them which had seen Him after He was risen" (Mark 16:14). We cannot expect to claim the promise in verse five if we are guilty of doubt as spoken of in verse six. We must "ask in faith."

There are reasons, other than unbelief, why our prayers are not answered, but they cannot be listed at this time. Suffice it to say, "If we ask any thing according to His will, He heareth us" (1 John 5:14).

Only God is completely trustworthy. Each one of us has at some time put faith in some person who has failed us, but God has never proved unfaithful to any one of us.

The word "wavering" in verse six is rendered "doubting." No Christian is more restless than when he is wavering. Like the billows of the sea driven with the wind and tossed, he is never settled, now in the depths and then on the heights, never unswerving. Like a vessel, tossed about, driven here and there, seeking advice first from this person, then another, he falls an easy prey to false teachers. Such restless Christians are "carried about with every wind of doctrine" (Eph. 4:14). The doubter receives much, and often confusing, advice from men, but, as verse seven tells us, he never receives anything from the Lord.

Oh, dear Christian, why do we doubt? Actually we have no reason for doing so. Do we believe that God possesses all wisdom, including that which we need? Do we believe He is able to impart His wisdom to us at all times? If we do, then why should we doubt? Let us come to our heavenly Father with believing hearts and count on His wisdom for life's every experience.

My Father is rich in houses and lands,
He holdeth the wealth of the world in His hands
Of rubies and diamonds, of silver and gold,
His coffers are full, He has riches untold.

My Father's own Son, the Saviour of men,
Once wandered on earth as the poorest of them;
But now He is pleading our pardon on high,
That we may be His when He comes by and by.

I once was an outcast stranger on earth,
A sinner by choice and an alien by birth;
But I've been adopted, my name's written down,
An heir to a mansion, a robe, and a crown.

A tent or a cottage, why should I care?
They're building a palace for me over there;
Tho' exiled from home, yet, still I may sing:
All glory to God, I'm a child of the King.

I'm a child of the King,
A child of the King,
With Jesus my Saviour
I'm a child of the King.

RICHES THROUGH
POVERTY

James 1:9-11

9. Let the brother of low degree rejoice in that he is exalted:

10. But the rich, in that he is made low: because as the flower of the grass he shall pass away.

11. For the sun is no sooner risen with a burning heat, but it withereth the grass, and the flower thereof falleth, and the grace of the fashion of it perisheth: so also shall the rich man fade away in his ways.

Forming another strange paradox, these three verses speak simultaneously of poverty and wealth, the two extremes of life, and how the true child of God should face each of them. In case God will permit some of us to prosper in this world, let us stir ourselves to learn what our attitude toward worldly possessions ought to be. Contrariwise, the right attitude is likewise important in that you may be one whom God will never permit to accumulate this world's goods.

Before we look at these conditions separately let us examine them briefly together. In both, the believer is exhorted to rejoice, and the reasons are given; but that in which one is to rejoice is directly opposite from that in which the other is to rejoice. The Christian of low degree is to rejoice in that he is exalted, but the rich, in that he is made low. Strange language, this! But the Bible contains other paradoxes equally as strange to the natural mind:

"As deceivers, and yet true;

"As unknown, and yet well known;

"As dying, and, behold, we live;

"As chastened, and not killed;

"As sorrowful, yet alway rejoicing;

"As poor, yet making many rich;

"As having nothing, and yet possessing all things" (2 Cor. 6:8-10).

"When I am weak, then am I strong" (2 Cor. 12:10).

"He that is greatest among you shall be your servant.

"And whosoever shall exalt himself shall be abased; and he that shall humble himself shall be exalted" (Matt. 23:11, 12).

James is telling us in verse nine that the brother of low degree is to rejoice in that he is exalted. Most professing Christians of my acquaintance complain if they cannot get ahead. Now why do we do this? Simply because we have lost sight of our real calling and dignity in Christ. A Christian who is lacking in material things has undiminishing possessions in Jesus Christ.

The "low degree" of which James writes is human appraisal; in Christ the believer possesses more than the wealthiest of this world without Christ. A Christian may be of inferior degree financially, socially, or racially; but he need not be moved by his standing according to man's standard. God's standard does not go by one's place, or face, or race in this life. Every saved person can rejoice because his name is written in heaven (Luke 10:20). Beloved child of God, "ye are a chosen generation, a royal priesthood . . ." (1 Peter 2:9). We are of God's royal family and therefore heirs of His kingdom. Beware lest any trial of poverty work a moral injury upon us.

I am willing to concede that, for my part, I have found it easier in the past to rejoice when wealth comes than when it goes. And I confess that this failure was the result of a worse failure: namely, the inexcusable ignorance of my position and possessions in Jesus Christ. The "brother of low degree," that is, the person of humble position in this life, should rejoice in the elevated position to which the grace of God has brought him.

No man comes too poor for the Lord Jesus to save. He said: "The Spirit of the Lord is upon Me, because He hath anointed Me to preach the Gospel to the poor . . ." (Luke 4:18). The Gospel invitation says: "Ho, every one that thirsteth, come ye to the waters, and he that hath no money; come ye, buy, and eat; yea, come, buy wine and milk without money and without price" (Isa. 55:1).

You see, the gospel of the grace of God has a leveling effect. To a poor, blind beggar our Lord said: "Arise." To rich Zacchaeus He said: "Come down." "The rich shall not give more, and the poor shall not give less" (Exod. 30:15). This was the law of God concerning the ransom of souls in the Old Testament times.

The moment a believing sinner trusts Jesus Christ for salvation he becomes God's child, "And if children, then heirs; heirs of God, and joint-heirs with Christ; if so be that we suffer with Him, that we may be also glorified together" (Rom. 8:17). The poor in this world's goods who trust in Jesus Christ have a standing before God equal to the richest saints. The redemption price for the poor man's soul was just as great as that for the wealthiest sinner, not ". . . silver and gold . . . but with the precious blood of Christ" (1 Peter 1:18, 19).

Dear brother or sister in Christ, the work you can do for God is just as necessary and fruit-bearing as that of the rich man, possibly more so. God needs someone to do the common tasks. All of us cannot afford to pay others to do the lesser tasks in the Lord's work. I know a wealthy Christian who will never soil his hands if he can avoid it. In a community door-to-door canvass for the purpose of distributing Gospel literature, he will assist in the purchase of tracts and even pay someone to distribute them, but he himself has never been known to assist personally in the actual work. We do not pass judgment; we illustrate. Let the brother of low degree rejoice that God has counted him worthy to serve in any capacity, whether it be cleaning the church building, passing out tracts, or ministering to the poor. The lowliest servant of Jesus Christ is an honored and exalted saint in God's eyes.

Many lowly men, poor in this world's goods, have been exalted by God above the rich in this life. A maintenance worker in a factory, a devoted Christian and respected deacon in the local church, invited the factory superintendent to attend services on the Lord's day. The prosperous employer accepted the invitation, and upon attending the worship service, saw his laboring employee occupying an exalted position of officiating minister at the Lord's table. It is not uncommon to see a servant in this world exalted above his master in spiritual matters.

Before examining James's comment of the rich man I feel constrained to look at two passages dealing with our Lord Jesus Christ, who said: "I am meek and lowly in heart" (Matt. 11:29). We read: "He humbled Himself, and became obedient unto death, even the death of the cross. Wherefore God also hath highly exalted Him, and given Him a name which is above every name" (Phil. 2:8, 9). Give thought to it! The royal Son of God stripped Himself of the glory of His majesty and voluntarily became the Father's bond-slave. Yes, and ours. He said: "I am among you as He that serveth" (Luke 22:27). He served God well, and us, when He "became obedient unto death, even the death of the cross." Notice, He humbled Himself, but He did not exalt Himself. "Wherefore God also hath highly exalted Him." For the Lord of glory the way up was down. And it is the way for each of us. "Let this mind be in you." J. H. Pickford writes: "This pattern of Jesus leaves us no choice; we must be God's nothings if God is going to do something through us. Let us step down from the throne of self and He will exalt us in due time." "Let the brother of low degree rejoice."

Poverty can produce great riches according to 2 Corinthians 8:9: "For ye know the grace of our Lord Jesus Christ, that, though He was rich, yet for your sakes He became poor, that ye through His poverty might be rich." This verse is closely related in meaning to the passage just considered in Philippians. Had he remained in heaven our blessed Lord would not have made many rich, but in coming He brought to every needy sinner God's riches—"the riches of His *goodness*" (Rom. 2:4), "the riches of His *grace*" (Eph. 1:7), and the "riches of His *glory*" (Eph.

3:16). He descended so low and gave so freely that He exhausted Himself and impoverished Himself of all His riches. But nothing was lost. We have been the recipients of all He relinquished. This is the strange paradox of obtaining riches through poverty.

The believer's wealth can never be calculated in dollars. We are rich in peace, righteousness, and hope; and neither adversity nor ill-health can take such wealth away from us. It is all because He became poor. "Let the brother of low degree rejoice."

James turns now to the rich: "But the rich, in that he is made low." This thought borders on contempt of wealth. James warns the rich man throughout the Epistle (2:2-6; 5:1-6). Somehow I cannot bring myself to disagree with James, since the perils of wealth are quite obvious.

Paul writes: "Charge them that are rich in this world, that they be not highminded, nor trust in uncertain riches, but in the living God, who giveth us richly all things to enjoy" (1 Tim. 6:17). But let the Bible speak about wealth and the wealthy. One of the snares into which the wealthy fall so often is their confidence in their riches rather than in the Lord, so that they become possessed by their possessions.

Wealth makes it difficult for a man to humble himself; it makes him a target for Satan to attack with pride and a sense of superiority. If any read these lines who are rich in this world's goods, remember that you have nothing you did not receive. Everything you possess came by the mercy of God. I warn you not to trust in your riches. They are uncertain. What you have today may be gone tomorrow. "Riches certainly make themselves wings; they fly away as an eagle" (Prov. 23:5). Our Lord said: "How hardly shall they that have riches enter into the kingdom of God" (Mark 10:23)! Few rich people are sufficiently humbled to be saved. A rich young man had come to Christ in quest of eternal life. He had inherited wealth but not eternal salvation. What he possessed was only temporal and he knew it. The Lord put him to the test to see if he was willing to lay aside his temporal goods to get eternal life. But the young man was sad and went away grieved, "for he had great possessions" (verse 22). Then Jesus, taking in the entire group in a single glance, said: "With what difficulty shall they who have riches enter into the kingdom of God!"

Satan places many varied barriers in the way of all who would be saved. In this instance the barrier was money. Then our Lord added: "It is easier for a camel to go through the eye of a needle, than for a rich man to enter into the kingdom of God." Our Lord does not declare it impossible for a wealthy person to be saved, but He is stating that it is difficult to get him saved. The hyperbole of the camel and the needle's eye teaches that he whose love of riches keeps him from submitting trustfully to Jesus Christ cannot be saved.

Another Biblical example of the teaching of James is to be found in our Lord's account of the rich man and the beggar (Luke 16:19-31). The poor beggar named Lazarus died, and his soul was carried by the angels of God to be with the believing dead who had died in the Lord, not because he was poor, but rather because he was a believer. The rich man died also and went to hell and conscious torment, not because he was rich, but because he would not believe. With great difficulty does a man with riches enter into the kingdom of God.

Returning now to James we hear him speak to the wealthy believer telling him to rejoice "in that he is made low." For a Jew to accept Jesus Christ meant that he would be dispossessed of any and all inheritance, cut off completely from loved ones as though he were dead. Such practice is not uncommon in our day. Paul testified: "Yea doubtless, and I count all things but loss for the excellency of the knowledge of Christ Jesus my Lord: for whom I have suffered the loss of all things, and do count them but dung, that I may win Christ" (Phil. 3:8). The mighty Saul of Tarsus was brought low; but he rejoiced, for in losing any earthly prestige and possessions, he gained eternal riches in Jesus Christ.

When a wealthy person becomes saved, he, like any other

Christian, is called to a life of separation. He does not at once step out of a wealthy class of the unsaved into a wealthy class of saved persons. If his heart is right with God, he discovers that in Christ he is no higher than the poorest of his brethren in Christ.

Now why should the rich man rejoice in that he is made low? "Because as the flower of the grass he shall pass away." When death comes he will be as the poor man. Both must leave everything behind when that last hour strikes. A lovely flower does not bloom forever, for its life and loveliness are soon gone. It is beautiful while it lasts but its life span is short. Riches may be useful in this life, but death severs a man and his wealth forever. Let the rich Christian rejoice in his eternal wealth in Christ only.

Since James will have more in his Epistle to say about money, let us conclude with a comment on verse 11. He writes: "For the sun is no sooner risen with a burning heat, but it withereth the grass, and the flower thereof falleth, and the grace of the fashion of it perisheth: so also shall the rich man fade away in his ways." As grass and flowers are scorched and wilted by a hot, dry wind (see Jonah 4:8; Matt. 13:6; Luke 12:55), so will the rich man and his riches fade away from this earthly scene.

There is a *way* which seemeth right unto man and with many it is the way of accumulating wealth, but the one who pursues *that* way must "fade away" in his purposes and pursuits to get richer. As the sweetness and beauty go from a fading flower, so is the wretched end of the rich man who forgets God. His plans and projects go unfinished. His hopes perish. The true child of God possesses an inheritance "incorruptible, and undefiled, and that fadeth not away, reserved in heaven" (1 Peter 1:4). The rich man, as a rich man, fades away as do his riches; the Christian, as a Christian, and his inheritance never fade. Life at its best is brief and uncertain. "Labour not for the meat which perisheth, but for that meat which endureth unto everlasting life, which the Son of man shall give unto you: for Him hath God the Father sealed" (John 6:27).

Yield not to temptation,
    For yielding is sin;
Each victory will help you
    Some other to win;
Fight manfully onward,
    Dark passions subdue;
Look ever to Jesus,
    He'll carry you through.

Shun evil companions,
    Bad language disdain;
God's name hold in reverence,
    Nor take it in vain;
Be thoughtful and earnest,
    Kindhearted and true;
Look ever to Jesus,
    He'll carry you through.

To him that o'ercometh,
    God giveth a crown;
Thro' faith we will conquer,
    Though often cast down;
He who is our Saviour,
    Our strength will renew;
Look ever to Jesus,
    He'll carry you through.

Ask the Saviour to help you,
Comfort, strengthen, and keep you;
He is willing to aid you,
He will carry you through.

SIN THROUGH
LUST AND LURE

James 1:13, 14

13. Let no man say when he is tempted, I am tempted of God: for God cannot be tempted with evil, neither tempteth he any man:

14. But every man is tempted, when he is drawn away of his own lust, and enticed.

These two verses take up an important theological question: namely, the origin of sin with the human race. James commences with the emphatic admonition that no man is ever to blame God when he is tempted to do wrong. If he should ever entertain such a thought, let him never say it. The tempting here, unlike that in verse 2, speaks of the solicitation of man to do evil. Now there have been those religious leaders who reasoned that since God permitted man to be in such a circumstance where he was exposed to temptation to do wrong, God was the author of the sin to which those circumstances had led. James warns us never to say such a thing.

Doing the very thing that we are warned here not to do is common among us all. For example, we excuse our wrongdoing on the ground of some inheritance or environment which we reason to be related to the providence of God, which we therefore conclude must of necessity come from God. It was this very reasoning to which our first parents resorted after the fall and it comes only from an unregenerate or carnal mind. Adam sought to excuse himself when he said to God: "The woman whom Thou gavest to be with me, she gave me of the tree, and I did eat" (Gen. 3:12). Did not God give him the woman who gave him the forbidden fruit? In its finality he was blaming God for his sin.

The one restriction that God had placed upon our first parents was reasonable, being a test of their faith and obedience, not a temptation to do wrong. The power of choice lay with them, and they had as much power to choose the good as they had to choose the evil. God did not compel Adam and Eve to eat the fruit; He forbade them, and yet Adam sought to blame the Lord.

A look at the Scriptures and then at the world shows us that man is not what his Creator intended him to be. Man is far from what he was when he came from the hands of his Creator. Are we to assume then that man sinned because he was made of defective material? No, never! "God created man in His own image . . . and God saw everything that he had made, and, behold, it was very good" (Gen. 1:27, 31). Adam was created a righteous and holy being and placed in a perfect environment entirely suited to his nature, so that he could not blame God for defection in himself or in his environment.

"God cannot be tempted with evil, neither tempteth He any man." It is unreasonable to conceive how any one who has not been first tempted himself by evil could tempt another to do evil. It would seem that a man who would shrink from the thought of God's doing evil must shrink also from the thought of His tempting man to do evil. He who is perfect in righteousness and holiness cannot be the originator of sin. A tempter to sin must be himself open to sin's temptations. God cannot be thus tempted. No man is ever driven to sin by the circumstances in which God has placed him. The poor man cannot blame his dishonesty on poverty. The drunkard cannot blame his drunkenness on the associates who gave him his first drink. Let us never excuse our wrongdoing by blaming the providence of God. There is absolutely nothing in the divine nature that responds to evil. God is righteous, hence He leads only in paths of righteousness. (Psalm 23:3).

Our Lord Jesus Christ, the God-Man, proved He could not be tempted to do evil, and Satan calculated wrong when he figured that Jesus Christ the Man could be tempted to sin. Not one of Satan's offers appealed to our Lord. Jesus Christ "knew no sin" (2 Cor. 5:21); He was "without sin" (Heb. 4:15); "separate from sinners" (Heb. 7:26); and "in Him is no sin" (1 John 3:5).

How then did sin enter the human race? James gives a reasonable and satisfying answer twofold in content. Temptation is both internal and external. Temptation may come from within when a man "*is drawn away of his own lust*," and it may come from without when he is "*enticed.*" From within it is *lust;* from without it is *lure.*

Temptation is traced first to our *lusts,* or *desires.* Where there is no desire there is no temptation. Not all persons have the same evil desires. An evil which may be desirable to one person may be repulsive to another. We are sometimes critical of others who have evil desires which may not bother us, forgetting that we have evil desires which may not appeal to them.

We do not always have an opportunity to fulfil our wrong desires; but when the opportunity does come, the real temptation comes also. God does not hold us chargeable when a desire to do wrong arises within, but we are answerable when that desire breaks through every barrier and takes advantage of the opportunity to sin.

Man's sinful, fallen nature is bent to do evil. We are shapen in iniquity and conceived in sin (Psalm 51:5). Thoughts and acts of sin spring from a principle or sin nature. The human heart is naturally deceitful and sick (Jer. 17:9), and out of it come forth evil thoughts (Matt. 15:19). A corrupt tree can only bring forth evil fruit (Matt. 7:17, 18). We all must agree with Paul where he says: "Sin . . . dwelleth in me" (Rom. 7:17). "If we say that we have no sin, we deceive ourselves, and the truth is not in us" (1 John 1:8).

How such an evil bent came to be is not our problem here.

Frankly, its origin does not matter. All desire to do wrong grows out of a depravity within man. Sin is not eternal, but it originated in the human race in the free act of Adam. Through one sin of this one man, Adam, a sinful nature is imputed to all of Adam's posterity, since he is the federal head and representative of the human race. Every man is tempted when he is drawn away by his own desires.

James also deals with the external allurement to do wrong in his use of the words "and enticed." The flesh with its evil desires is the internal foe; Satan with his enticements is the external foe. The believer must be on guard at all times. A fifth column operates from within while the enemy solicits from without. Our Lord said to His own: "Watch and pray, that ye enter not into temptation: the spirit indeed is willing, but the flesh is weak" (Matt. 26:41).

Were it not for our desires within, Satan could never gain a victory over us by his enticements. Our Lord was enticed by Satan to sin, but Christ could not fall prey to Satan's enticements since He had no lust within. The Scripture says that He "was in all points tempted like as we are, yet without sin" (Heb. 4:15). This means that He was tempted in all points like ourselves, apart from indwelling sin. He was solicited to sin by Satan and the Scribes and Pharisees, but He did not submit to speak or act wrongly, because He could not. He revolted against sin and rejected every offer to commit sin because there was nothing carnal in Him to respond to temptation. His temptations never sprang, as in our case, from any sinful desire on His part. The temptations, or enticements, from without left His sinless nature undisturbed and unscarred.

Satan can break through the defenses of a fallen sinner, but he could break through our perfect Saviour never. We are not suggesting that our Lord Jesus was able *not to sin,* but that He was *not able to sin.* There never was any inclination in Christ to do any of the wrong things He was tempted to do. It is the sinner, therefore, who needs the help.

Viewing the awful consequences of sin which James clearly states, and which we shall take up in our next study, we should come to our "great high priest, that is passed into the heavens, Jesus the Son of God" (Heb. 4:14). He is able to sympathize. Mark well, He does not sympathize with our sins. We need never look to Him for sympathy if we yield to sin. True, Christ is our judicial advocate with the Father if we do sin (1 John 2:1), and "If we confess our sins, He is faithful and just to forgive us our sins, and to cleanse us from all unrighteousness" (1 John 1:9). But having been attacked from without by Satan, and thus having passed through the path of temptation, He feels for us. The Scripture says He is *"touched."* What tenderness! What compassion! He knows what it means to be tempted. He understands the fierceness of Satan's attacks.

"Let us therefore come boldly unto the throne of grace, that we may obtain mercy, and find grace to help in time of need" (Heb. 4:16). Are you being tempted from within or enticed from without? Come to the Saviour! Have you yielded to temptation? Come to the Saviour! Confess all to Him now. As we watch and pray at the throne of grace we shall not yield to temptation. If you have yielded to temptation, you need mercy; if you confess your sin to Him, divine mercy will be extended to you. If you are being tempted, you need grace to resist evil, and as you come to Him grace will be extended to you. He hates the sin, but loves the sinner. While there is still time, and before it is too late, "let us come."

What though th' accuser roar
    Of ills that I have done;
I know them well, and thousands more;
    Jehovah findeth none.

His be the Victor's name
    Who fought our fight alone;
Triumphant saints no honor claim;
    Their conquest was His own.

By weakness and defeat,
    He won the meed and crown;
Trod all our foes beneath His feet,
    By being trodden down.

He hell in hell laid low;
    Made sin, He sin o'erthrew;
Bowed to the grave, destroyed it so,
    And death, by dying, slew.

Bless, bless the Conqueror slain!
    Slain by divine decree!
Who lived, who died, who lives again,
    For thee, His saint, for thee.

DEATH THROUGH
SIN

James 1:15-17

15. Then when lust hath conceived, it bringeth forth sin; and sin, when it is finished, bringeth forth death.

16. Do not err, my beloved brethren.

17. Every good gift and every perfect gift is from above, and cometh down from the Father of lights, with whom is no variableness, neither shadow of turning.

Having dealt with the causes of sin in verses 13 and 14, James continues with the all-important subject of the inevitable consequences of sin, namely, death. If we fail to come to God's throne of grace in the moment of temptation, but instead yield to some evil desire, "Then when lust hath conceived, it bringeth forth sin." And lest any one should minimize sin, as many do, the apostle wants all to know the progress of sin. He traces it quite simply: *lust—sin—death.*

Any act of sin, which is any transgression against the holiness and the laws of God, must run its natural course—it "bringeth forth death." The sin does not end with the speaking of an evil word or the committing of an evil deed. It must of necessity yield its inevitable fruit. So say the laws of God, and no man has ever dared to defy those laws and prove them inoperative. Death follows sin as naturally, and by as perpetual and permanent a law, as night follows day.

This law of death through sin was introduced by God to the first man of His creation. God said to Adam: "But of the tree of the knowledge of good and evil, thou shalt not eat of it: for in the day that thou eatest thereof thou shalt surely die" (Gen. 2:17). Adam sinned in willful disobedience. At the moment of his sin spiritual death entered, and with it exemption from bodily death was forfeited also. Before the fall the human body was capable of immortality, but after Adam sinned it was impossible for him not to die. And since Adam was both the federal and organic representative of the human race, death of necessity fastened itself upon every one of his descendants. The fall had to be universal, extending to all of Adam's posterity (Rom. 5:12-21; 1 Cor. 15:21). The law cannot be broken; "It is appointed unto men once to die" (Heb. 9:27).

But how does death through sin apply to believers? James addressed himself primarily to Christians. The Bible, both Old and New Testaments, contains a number of illustrations showing to us how sin brings death to the child of God. Now we are certain that there is now no condemnation to them which are in Christ Jesus (Rom. 8:1); that is, no person who has been born again can suffer eternal separation from God in hell, which is the second death (Rev. 21:8). However, it is clear from several passages in the Bible that even Christians are punished with physical death because of willful sin. Such deaths are not accidental but divinely intentional. God has struck men dead who persisted in sinning against Him. He killed Nadab and Abihu when they offered strange fire before Him (Lev. 10:1, 2). He killed Ananias and Sapphira when they lied to Him (Acts 5:10). He kills Christians who persist in partaking of the Lord's Supper in an unworthy manner (1 Cor. 11:30). The Apostle John warns the believer that "There is a sin unto death" (1 John 5:16).

Let not any one of us ever set himself as a judge in these matters by concluding that the early death of a Christian is the judgment of God for sin. God alone is the Judge and He only has full knowledge. But let the law of death through sin serve as a solemn warning to all who claim to be Christian. We ought never to tamper with any of God's laws, certainly not with the law which says that "the wages of sin is death" (Rom. 6:23).

Now we all know that sin has its pleasures. The writer to the Hebrews tells us that Moses acknowledged this, but Moses knew also the excitement and gratification which sinful indulgences afford are but "for a season" (Heb. 11:25). To those who live the longest, and enjoy the pleasures of sin to the fullest possible extent, death comes at last and cuts off all the streams of lustful pleasures.

Let a man weigh the pleasures of sin, which are but for a season, with an endless eternity of regret, remorse, and the bitter agonies of divine retribution, and he will make the wise choice to stand with Jesus Christ and the people of God. Before you sin, weigh the recompense of the reward for sin (Heb. 11:26).

Faith can be sure that God will recompense a fair reward commensurate with the reproach that a believer must suffer in this life, for it was by faith that Moses refused the pleasures of Egypt and chose rather to suffer affliction and reproach. Moses renounced those things for which the heart of the natural man craves, those things that are temporal, visible, and satisfying to the lusts of the flesh, and to them he never turned back because he beheld Him who is invisible. Just as sure as we are that sin pays its wages, so sure are we that God will reward those who turn from sin to Jesus Christ.

"Do not err, my beloved brethren." James adds here that we are to make no mistake about these things. There is a question as to whether this verse (16) goes with what precedes it or with the statement which follows. It could well apply to both. We are to make no mistake about the origin of sin (verses 13, 14) or the result of sin (verse 15). Rather we must be exceedingly cautious not to be deceived in these matters.

The sin question, with all of its many implications and ramifications, is perhaps one about which more people are deceived than any other. Many persons have a false idea that they can cast all restraint to the winds and live as they please, expecting God in the end to show mercy. If this book is being read by any person with such ideas, let me pass on to you God's warning: "Be not deceived; God is not mocked: for whatsoever a man soweth, that shall he also reap" (Gal. 6:7). "Do not err, my beloved brethren."

Verse 17 mentions another fact about which we are not to err, namely, God is the Author of all that is good. Solicitation to do wrong comes from men and Satan but never from God. He is not the source of our sins and sufferings. Behind every mercy and blessing stands God, the Giver of every good and perfect gift. He is a great Giver.

There is an interesting thought in the use of the word "gift" in this verse. In the Greek these words are not the same. The first word for gift is *"dosis"* and is translated "act of giving." The second usage of the word is *"dorema,"* and is translated as the noun "gift." The thought here is rich and beautiful. Both the act of giving and the gift are good. The act of giving would seem to include both the motive and the measure. When God gives, He has no ulterior motive such as giving to receive again. I am not too sure that the motive for our giving gifts at Christmas time is always good. How often have we scurried about at the last minute for a gift for someone only because we received an unexpected gift from that person! How many names have we added to our Christmas card mailing list of those persons who have sent us cards! When God gives, it is "liberally" (1:5), and that with no thought of receiving anything in return. He gave *first* out of love for man (John 3:16). His daily benefits, like food, clothing, shelter, strength of body, soundness of mind, and mercies too numerous to mention here come from His bountiful heart and hand.

The Apostle Paul wrote: "He that spared not His own Son, but delivered Him up for us all, how shall He not with Him also freely give us all things?" (Rom. 8:32). Yes, our heavenly Father has given to us *all* things—His Son, His Spirit, His Word, and His very own life. Every day should be a day of thanksgiving for the child of God.

We have never been charged for one single mercy or blessing, nor have we merited one. James tells us that all blessings come "from above." The expression "from above" is found many times throughout the Scriptures. Our Lord used it when He spoke to Nicodemus about the new birth. He said: "Except a man be born *from above*" (John 3:3). The word is *anothen,* translated "from above." The new birth is not of this earth, but from another world, from above, even from the heart of God. Our heavenly Father is the source of every good thing.

Here God is called *"the Father of lights."* I take it that this refers to the great luminaries, the sun, the moon, and the stars. Some of these magnificent heavenly bodies are essential to man's existence, while others may only add to the beauty of God's universe. He has created them all for our blessing, and they are among His "perfect" gifts. With Him there is no "variableness," that is, no changeableness. God is not capricious and changeable like man. We are vacillating, variable, veering—but God is not. For God's unchangeableness we should be thankful every day of our lives. Praise the Lord for His consistency and constancy. With the Father of Lights there is no variableness.

James adds, ". . . neither shadow of turning." The American Standard Version, and other versions, translate this expression "neither shadow that is cast by turning." We have observed an eclipse of the sun as it has been obscured by the moon. This is a shadow caused by turning.

God is the Author of light, and with Him is no darkness at all, not so much as a shadow. The dark shadows that bring their gloom and sadness to the human heart come from an earthly source. When we allow anything to come between God and us, we must walk in the shadows without the light of His countenance. But He has not changed. He does not cast the shadows. If there are shadows without the Light, it is because we have turned our faces from Him, thereby causing them ourselves. Let us behold Him daily in the beauty of holiness that we may experience the light of His presence and reflect that Light to others.

Holy Bible, Book divine,
Precious treasure, thou art mine;
Mine to tell me whence I came;
Mine to teach me what I am;

Mine to chide me when I rove;
Mine to show a Saviour's love;
Mine thou art to guide and guard;
Mine to punish or reward;

Mine to comfort in distress,
Suffering in this wilderness;
Mine to show, by living faith,
Man can triumph over death;

Mine to tell of joys to come,
And the rebel sinner's doom;
O thou holy Book divine,
Precious treasure, thou art mine.

LIFE THROUGH
THE WORD

James 1:18-20

18. Of his own will begat he us with the word of truth, that we should be a kind of firstfruits of his creatures.

19. Wherefore, my beloved brethren, let every man be swift to hear, slow to speak, slow to wrath.

20. For the wrath of man worketh not the righteousness of God.

The subject before us is one of the most blessed in Chapter One. This truth, namely, Regeneration, the imparting of divine life through the Word, is one of unspeakable importance. Actually this is the Bible's major message. The salvation of man is that purpose for which Christ came. He said as much in Luke 19:10. This is a vast subject and understandable only through its several aspects: Regeneration, Redemption, Justification, Sanctification, Repentance, Faith.

In verse 18 James takes up the subject of Regeneration. The word *regeneration* appears but two times in the Bible (Matt. 19:28; Titus 3:5, 6). In the passage in Matthew it means "a new order," referring to the millennium, Christ's kingdom on earth. In Titus Paul uses the word in reference to the spiritual aspect of the kingdom. It is the "new order," the "new creation," into which God places the believing sinner the moment he believes.

Regeneration may be defined as an act of God whereby He bestows upon the believing sinner new life. This life is God's own life. God Himself is the Bestower, the believer is but the recipient. Our Lord said it is impossible for a man to enter into the kingdom of God (the new order) except he be born again. Being "born again" (John 3:3), "born . . . of God" (John 1:13),

"Born . . . of the Spirit" (John 3:5) are expressions synonymous with being *regenerated*.

In speaking of the believer's new life in Christ, James writes: *"Of His own will begat He us."* This new life has its origin with God. He begat us. It is one of the perfect gifts from above of verse 17. If God did not will to save us, we could not possibly be saved. "Salvation is of the Lord" (Jonah 2:9). He "is . . . not willing that any should perish, but that all should come to repentance" (2 Peter 3:9).

God wants all men everywhere to be saved. He always has said to man, "I will"; but the sinner does not receive God's life until he too replies, "I will." God is saying, "I will if you will." This is the essential factor in the marriage ceremony. The marriage is not recognized until both the man and the woman say "I will." When Christ gave Himself for the Church (Eph. 5:25), He manifested the love of God, and that was the "I will" of God, without which man's "I will" would be useless. But oh, blessed truth that God said "I will" in the long ago!

James reminds us that it was first of "His [God's] own will" that a man is born from above. That God, of His own free will, should choose us to be heirs of eternal salvation through faith in His Son is the greatest marvel of all times. Eternal salvation is the apex of giving. God fashioned and finished redemption by His own will. We are born again, begotten, brought forth from the dead, not "of the will of the flesh, nor of the will of man, but of God" (John 1:13).

The Revised Version translates the words "begat He us" to read, "brought us forth." The construction of the Greek is participial, and reads: "Willing He brought us forth." Induced by no other reason, God willingly brought us forth out of death into life (John 5:24). In verse 15 James uses the term "bringeth forth." The lust and sin are seen bringing "forth death"; here God, through His Word, begets life.

The Apostle is careful to mention next the *instrument* of Regeneration: *"the Word of truth."* The "Word of truth" is the whole system of Christian truth found within the confines of the Bible. It is the Word of God, the gospel of Jesus Christ. Plumptre writes: "It is something more than the written Word of the Old Testament Scriptures, or even the spoken word of preachers. It is the whole message from God to man, of which the written or spoken word is but one of the channels, and which to those who receive it rightly is the beginning of a higher life."

We cannot say too much about the necessity of the preeminence of God's Word in the Christian ministry. The use of "Christian films" and "gospel magic" may have a place in some phase of Christian activity, but they are a poor substitute for the teaching and preaching of God's Word. "For the *Word of God* is quick, and powerful, and sharper than any twoedged sword, piercing even to the dividing asunder of soul and spirit, and of the joints and marrow, and is a discerner of the thoughts and intents of the heart" (Heb. 4:12).

The Word of God includes the whole of God's verbal communications to man, and I believe this to be the idea that James attaches to the phrase. God's Word is "quick": that is, living, active, not a dead letter but a living and life-giving spirit. Proclaim it with accuracy and clarity and in the power of the Holy Spirit, and it is certain to work in all who believe (1 Thess. 2:13).

There is a principle, or call it a law, which says that all good seed brought in contact with moist earth will produce and develop life. So with the good seed of the Word of God. In it there is a potency resident that, when received into the good ground of a believing heart, will produce and develop life (Mark 4:3, 14, 20). The Apostle Peter wrote: "Being born again, not of corruptible seed, but of incorruptible, by the Word of God, which liveth and abideth for ever" (1 Peter 1:23). The Bible is doubtless the one instrument used to bring to pass the greatest revival and revolutionary movements for good in world history. James is but repeating the words of the Lord Jesus when he writes that we are brought forth (begotten) with the word of truth (John 5:24). Paul does likewise when he adds: "So then faith cometh by hearing, and hearing by the Word of God" (Rom. 10:17). Only living things can produce life.

Since the Bible is a living Book, it is likewise a life-giving Book. This is a mystery not easy to explain, just as there is mystery attached to life in general that the most clever biologist cannot explain; but we are certain that the Bible works. The writer, at the time of this writing, is in his sixteenth year as pastor in the same church. He has sought to preach and teach the Word of God faithfully and has seen it work miracles in the transformation of hundreds of lives. "So shall My Word be that goeth forth out of My mouth: it shall not return unto Me void, but it shall accomplish that which I please, and it shall prosper in the thing whereto I sent it" (Isa. 55:11).

The Apostle includes God's purpose in regeneration: *"that we should be a kind of firstfruits of His creatures."* To understand the meaning of this term, I suggest we look together at an Old Testament ceremony practiced by Israel. In connection with the Passover celebration, the Israelite presented to the Lord the firstfruits of the harvest. It was an act of consecration in which the offering of the part was a pledge of the whole. The worshiper was acknowledging that it all came from the Lord, hence all belonged to Him (Lev. 23:9-14). Just as soon as Israel arrived in the land flowing with milk and honey and gathered the first harvest, God was to have His portion first (Lev. 23:14; Deut. 26:1, 2). The land did not belong to them. It was God's possession and they were holding it in trust for Him. The believer is to recognize the principle of divine ownership in everything he possesses.

Now when a believing sinner is regenerated he is not his own. Having been bought with a price he becomes the purchased possession of the One who redeemed him (1 Cor. 6:19, 20). When God saves a man, giving him a new life, that life is God's possession, and the Christian is merely holding it in trust for its Owner.

We must recognize the principle of divine ownership in all

that we possess. All that we are and have are God's. When I consecrate my first waking moments to God in the morning, it is but a symbol and earnest that all of my time is at His disposal. When I commence my day by giving to my Lord the first expressions of adoration and affection, it is but a symbol and pledge that He has first claim upon my heart at all times. When I bring to God the firstfruits of all money He entrusts to my care, it is a symbol and promise that all which remains is at His disposal. This is a true recognition of the fundamental principle: namely, "All things come of Thee, and of Thine own have we given Thee" (1 Chron. 29:14). After all, He regenerated us and we are a kind of firstfruits.

It is written of the redeemed: "These were redeemed from among men, being the firstfruits unto God and to the Lamb" (Rev. 14:4). Of Old Testament saints we read: "Israel was holiness unto the Lord, and the firstfruits of His increase" (Jer. 2:3). May it ever be so of us!

"Wherefore, my beloved brethren, let every man be swift to hear, slow to speak, slow to wrath" (James 1:19). At first glance it might seem that this verse introduces a sharp change of thought, yet it is not so sharp a change when examined more closely. It begins with the word "wherefore." The use of "wherefore" usually refers to something that has gone before. James has just stated the power of the Word in regeneration. God brings us forth out of spiritual death into life by His Word. Now because of this, let the "beloved brethren . . . be swift to hear." The exhortation is to alertness and alacrity to receive the truth of the Word of God. Our Lord said: "The sower soweth the Word . . . He that hath ears to hear, let him hear" (Mark 4:14, 9). (See also Revelation 2:7, 11, 29; 3:6, 13, 22.)

If the sinner wishes to have life, and the brethren wish to attain to the maturity of Christian manhood, "let every man be swift to hear." I fear that our times have produced a pace so fast and a multiplicity of attractions so appealing that men are not ready and eager to avail themselves of the many opportunities of increasing their acquaintance with the "Word of truth." The spoken and the written Word of God is available to every one of us. There are many cheap and trifling things in current conversation, newspapers, magazines, on television and radio in which we act wisely when we are *slow* to hear, but we need to be eager listeners and learners of those things that God would say to us.

Could it be that we are not more "swift to hear" because we are not "slow to speak"? God gave us two ears and only one mouth. Should we not be twice as swift to listen and learn? A wise man will listen to others and answer only if he is certain he has something worthwhile to say.

Some of us are blighted with the craving to be incessantly chattering. A proverb says "In the multitude of words there wanteth not sin: but he that refraineth his lips is wise" (Prov. 10:19). To refrain the lips is not always easy, but it is the better part of true wisdom. A tongue that is not still lacks the control of the discerning. A wise man is of a quiet spirit. "He that hath knowledge spareth his words: and a man of understanding is of an excellent spirit. Even a fool, when he holdeth his peace, is counted wise: and he that shutteth his lips is esteemed a man of understanding" (Prov. 17:27, 28). The Christian who is well taught in the "Word of truth" is slow to speak, for he knows that "every idle word that men shall speak, they shall give account thereof in the day of judgment. For by thy words thou shalt be justified, and by thy words thou shalt be condemned" (Matt. 12:36, 37).

The foregoing reference does not suggest that a man is justified on the ground of a good confession of words. Salvation is by grace through faith, and not through works or words of any description. But let all believers bear in mind at all times that we must all appear before the Judgment Seat of Christ to give an account of deeds done in the body (2 Cor. 5:10). The Christian, living according to the Word of God, will not utter useless, barren words.

"Wherefore . . . let every man be . . . *slow to wrath.*" From both personal experience and observation I think I know why James might have linked the two expressions "slow to speak, slow to wrath." We all are acquainted with the fact that words unfitly spoken often cause an outburst of temper. What starts out as a sincere and friendly discussion sometimes leads to an argument, with its resulting flare of anger. Among those things for which the Christian should seek wisdom (1:5), there is the ever-present need for a controlled tongue and a controlled temper. When we are "swift to hear" the Word of truth, we will be slow to become angry. The same Word which is able to save the sinner is likewise able to sanctify the saint (John 17:17). The hearer and doer of God's Word will practice self-control at all times.

The Scriptures never speak against a child of God's becoming righteously angry at sin. Contrariwise, the Bible says: "Ye that love the Lord, hate evil" (Psalm 97:10). One of the deficiencies among believers is the lack of concern and the loss of capacity to be aroused over evil. There is an anger which is not sin. It is stated by Paul where he writes: "Be ye angry, and sin not: let not the sun go down upon your wrath: Neither give place to the devil" (Eph. 4:26, 27). The indication here is that a believer can be angry apart from sinning. If I am angry at nothing but sin, I can be angry so as not to sin.

Now we must beware lest we excuse sheer temper by calling it righteous indignation. If a violent passion is aroused in my mind, accompanied by the desire to take vengeance or to obtain satisfaction from one who has offended me, and that passion is accompanied by a hidden malice or smouldering resentment in my heart, I have sinned. But there is that unhappy aftermath which always comes to those who are guilty of this sin: "A man of great wrath shall suffer punishment" (Prov. 19:19). One of the firstfruits of every newborn child of God is the subduing of every evil passion. Yet we have met not a few Christians who seem to be weak at this point. Anger and a bad temper cling to them.

Lest any reader treat lightly of this matter, let me illustrate further. As I write these lines there comes to mind an incident which occurred only recently. A young married man came to the study requesting membership in our assembly, but he felt that in all honesty I should know that he had been released recently from prison, having served two years for the crime of involuntary manslaughter. One day while at his work the foreman of his department issued an order of which my friend disapproved. An argument followed, words became heated, tempers flared, and fists flew. In the fracas the foreman was knocked to the floor, his head striking a sharp object, causing his death. The Christian man was tried in a court of law, found guilty, and sentenced to from two to twelve years in prison. After serving two years he was released for good behavior, but must remain on parole for ten years. He now has gotten victory over the sin of wrath, but at what a price! God had to put him in a prison cell for two years to teach him a lesson he might have learned more easily. Many murders proceed from wrath.

The Bible condemns sinful anger. Our Lord said: "Whosoever is angry with his brother without a cause shall be in danger of the judgment" (Matt. 5:22). The application of this verse for us is a warning against unwarranted anger with a fellow Christian which issues from pride and which desires the injury of the one against whom the anger is aimed. When Jesus went into the temple and beheld the money changers, He was angry with an anger that scorched and blistered; but His was not a selfish and vindictive anger expressed with contempt. The true children of God's kingdom are partakers of the divine nature, having been made righteous. They therefore love the brethren.

The Apostle Paul includes wrath as one of the works of the flesh (Gal. 5:20) and therefore must be "put away" (Eph. 4:31). There ought never to be any passionate outburst of anger or hostile feeling coming from a child of God. We must pray daily that God might set a guard at the door of our lips so that we might be slow to speak and slow to wrath. Remember, "A soft answer turneth away wrath: but grievous words stir up anger" (Prov. 15:1).

The Apostle now gives a reason why the believer must be slow to wrath. "For the wrath of man worketh not the righteousness of God" (James 1:20). The righteousness which God requires, that is, the righteous character of God that every man must behold in the children of God, is obscured when we become angry. Anger does not help the cause of our Lord Jesus Christ.

Our Lord once said to His disciples: "They shall put you out of the synagogues: yea, the time cometh, that whosoever killeth you will think that he doeth God service" (John 16:2). Here Christ is predicting that religious Jews will angrily persecute His followers, going as far as to murder them, feeling they were doing God service by their deeds of violence. Saul of Tarsus so persecuted Christians because he believed them heretical (Acts 8:1). These things he regretfully testified of later (Acts 26:9, 10). After Paul's conversion a fanatical and bloodthirsty band of more than forty conspired to kill him (Acts 23:12, 13). But such a display of man's wrath never shows forth the righteousness of God. When a man is unrighteously angry, it is not possible for him to speak and act righteously. An angry person is not fully rational and therefore says and does things he would never do in a quiet and thoughtful moment.

The anger of those Jews of whom our Lord spoke in John 16:2 prevails in those who hear God's Word but refuse to surrender to it. Their wrath was kindled because the disciples of Christ preached His Deity and Messiahship, which they rejected. How like some who attend our churches today and get angry when the plain truth of the Scriptures is taught! Cain rejected God's demand for a blood sacrifice; and when God rejected his offering, Cain in anger killed his brother (Gen. 4:1-8). Men get angry today when they hear the minister of God's Word say that there cannot possibly be salvation apart from the sacrificial death and resurrection of Jesus Christ. Actually all such do not get angry with man but with God Himself. Such anger does no one good. It does only eternal hurt.

Even Christians become angry when the preaching of God's Truth convicts them of some wrongdoing. I recall such anger early in my own Christian experience. I had joined a lodge where its members were made to swear to a secret oath. At that time I knew nothing of what the Bible taught about a child of God's becoming a member of a secret society. Then one day Evangelist Anthony Zeoli came to our community to conduct a series of preaching services. In a part of one message on the separation of Christians, he quoted more than a score of Bible references condemning such practices among believers. That night I became so angry I thought to myself I would never attend church again. But that message was just what I needed, and sometime during the ensuing year the Spirit of God convicted me greatly, and I then and there decided that I must withdraw from that secret society inasmuch as the Word of God condemned such affiliations for Christians.

It is God's design to produce practical righteousness in each of His children, but this can never be accomplished where anger is permitted to lay smoldering in the heart. The true Christian will be swift to listen to and learn the Word of Truth, and this in turn will crowd out the sin of anger. Does God see in each of us that holy character for which He longs? Let us remember at all times that wrath in a servant of Jesus Christ is a misrepresentation of His saving Gospel and is therefore out of place.

Awake, our souls; away, our fears;
    Let every trembling thought be gone;
Awake, and run the heavenly race,
    And put a cheerful courage on.

True, 'tis a strait and thorny road,
    And mortal spirits tire and faint;
But they forget the mighty God
    That feeds the strength of every saint—

Thee, mighty God whose matchless power
    Is ever new and ever young,
And firm endures, while endless years
    Their everlasting circles run.

From Thee, the overflowing spring,
    Our souls shall drink a fresh supply,
While such as trust their native strength
    Shall melt away, and droop, and die.

Swift as an eagle cuts the air,
    We'll mount aloft to Thine abode;
On wings of love our souls shall fly,
    Nor tire amidst the heavenly road.

BLESSING THROUGH
DOING

James 1:21-27

21. Wherefore lay apart all filthiness and superfluity of naughtiness, and receive with meekness the engrafted word, which is able to save your souls.

22. But be ye doers of the word, and not hearers only, deceiving your own selves.

23. For if any be a hearer of the word, and not a doer, he is like unto a man beholding his natural face in a glass:

24. For he beholdeth himself, and goeth his way, and straightway forgetteth what manner of man he was.

25. But whoso looketh into the perfect law of liberty, and continueth therein, he being not a forgetful hearer, but a doer of the work, this man shall be blessed in his deed.

26. If any man among you seem to be religious, and bridleth not his tongue, but deceiveth his own heart, this man's religion is vain.

27. Pure religion and undefiled before God and the Father is this, To visit the fatherless and widows in their affliction, and to keep himself unspotted from the world.

Where there is life there will be growth. Practical faith in the Word should naturally grow into practical obedience to the Word. That same "Word of Truth" that produces life is able to nourish and sustain life. Faith and obedience go hand in hand. One of our well-known hymns says: *"Trust and obey,* for there's no other way." By His Word God brought us forth out of death into life; by His Word He will show us how the new life must be lived. To trust the Word is to obey the Word.

The Bible is the only safe and sensible standard of right and wrong. Its precepts do not take the joy out of life; they make life worth living. To the believer in Jesus Christ, the Word of God is "the perfect law of liberty," not a code of "Do's" and "Don't's."

It is not a letter to which we are bound by fear, but instead it is the law of liberty written by the Spirit on the fleshy table of our hearts. The Christian does right because he wants to and loves and serves Him not by outward compulsion but by inward constraint. Soon we shall seek to show how the Word works in producing the desire and ability to measure up to the divine standard, but first look at the standard in verse 21.

"Wherefore lay apart all filthiness and superfluity of naughtiness." There is something the believer must lay apart, put away, pull out by the roots: namely, *naughtiness.* Our modern use of this word "naughtiness" causes me to hesitate to use it. We seldom ever use it today except to refer to some mild juvenile misdeed, but we have lost its real meaning. The Old English contained the general idea of wickedness, and all wickedness is filthy and superfluous. Every form of uncleanness whether in thought, word, or deed must be rooted out of the life of a Christian. This embodies the test of a good hearer of God's Word. If the tawdry things of life have not been put away, there is reason to question whether the Word that was heard has really brought forth new life. Not all who listen to the Word of God explained and who read the Bible get saved, and none but the truly saved clear away the foul rank growth of the old life.

The Bible says the human heart is "deceitful above all things, and desperately wicked" (Jer. 17:9). Our Lord Jesus said: "Out of the heart proceed evil thoughts, murders, adulteries, fornications, thefts, false witness, blasphemies" (Matt. 15:19). Dirty stories, filthy talk, cheap jokes with a double meaning are common among the unsaved who have not the Holy Spirit within, but the child of God who has received the nature of God is sensitive to grief caused by any lingering filthiness; therefore he will lay it aside. Filthy speech cannot be reconciled with the Holy Spirit.

How is God's standard attained? Only as we *"receive with meekness the engrafted Word."* We need to learn how to read the Bible and how to listen to others explain its truth. Too often we have a wrong attitude toward the Word as well as toward those who teach it, thus showing our own failure to deny self. Some persons who attend preaching services and Bible conferences show an unwillingness to surrender certain sins and selfish desires. Instead of receiving the Word meekly, they resist it proudly. The Word meekly received is bound to be immensely fruitful. Of those who put away filthy words and actions, our Lord says: "These are they which are sown on good ground; such as hear the word, and receive it, and bring forth fruit, some thirtyfold, some sixty, and some an hundred." (Mark 4:20). Only those profit by the Word who humbly submit to it.

James gives to us also the process by which the Word produces holiness. The statement *"the engrafted Word"* suggests a process of propagation. Only as the Word is really implanted does it become united with the heart. Unless the truth becomes rooted in us through faith, the fruit of righteousness cannot be brought forth. As the Word of God roots itself more deeply in us, the new life develops and the old life dies.

The figure of grafting used here is an interesting one. On one of my visits to Florida, a native of that state showed me a sturdy young lemon tree in his yard that bore delicious sweet oranges. He had grafted a bud from a cultivated orange tree into the lower trunk of the lemon tree. As soon as the bud started to grow, showing that it was receiving nourishment from the roots, my friend had cut off the trunk just above the engrafted bud, which continued to grow and eventually bore sweet fruit.

What a wonderful picture this is of the true Christian! God engrafts, or implants, His Word into these natural bodies. As we receive it with meekness, He infuses that Word into our very being and soon the sweetness and richness of the divine nature is produced in us.

And what a wonderful salvation the Word provides! James adds, which *"is able to save your souls."* This means that the implanted Word, meekly received, has in it the potency of salvation from the power of sin. Now keep in mind that the Apostle is not speaking in this verse to the unsaved. He is addressing the "beloved brethren" as is clearly seen in the context (1:16, 19).

James does not call upon the unsaved to lay apart all filthiness and superfluity of naughtiness, for the Bible nowhere appeals to an unsaved man to change his habits in order to be saved. The sinner must come to Christ, confess his sins, and receive salvation as God's free gift through the merit of Christ's atoning work in His death and resurrection. Not until he becomes saved does the sinner know anything of the power of the Word to overcome the practice of sin.

The salvation set forth in verse 21 is for the saved. Yes, the saved need to be saved. It is possible, my Christian brother, that you need to be saved right now from some unclean practice, from some defiling sin. If the word "soul" be rendered "life" the passage becomes clearer in its application to Christians. Our Lord said: "What shall it profit a man, if he shall gain the whole world, and lose his own *soul?*" (Mark 8:36). In the parallel passage in Luke's account, it reads: "For what is a man advantaged, if he gain the whole world, and lose *himself,* or be cast away?" (Luke 9:25). James, like our Lord, speaks of a man's natural life. God wants to save His children from the snares and pitfalls of sin in this present life. He desires to preserve the life of each of His children from every defiling thing, lest when we have confessed Christ to others we ourselves should become castaways.

The Apostle Paul sought to preserve his life from defilement in order that he might not lose the incorruptible crown in the day of the believer's judgment. He wrote: "And every man that striveth for the mastery is temperate in all things. Now they do it to obtain a corruptible crown; but we an incorruptible. I therefore so run, not as uncertainly; so fight I, not as one that beateth the air: But I keep under my body, and bring it into subjection: lest that by any means, when I have preached to others, I myself should be a castaway" (1 Cor. 9:25-27).

The contest against defilement is real. Paul treated his body, not as his master, but as his servant, lest, by any chance, after he had exhorted others, he might discover in the end that he was disqualified from the competition. We are not shadow boxing. The old man is real and active and wicked. The flesh is at war with the Spirit. The new man, by the implanted Word of God, must dictate to the old nature. Failure here spells failure in effective service for Jesus Christ, and failure in service will mean loss of rewards at the Judgment Seat of Christ. My brother, your refusal to obey the Word of God might not disqualify you as a Christian, but it certainly will disqualify you as a contestant for rewards. The sad condition of the church is the tragedy of its castaways, men and women who are failing in the matter of self-discipline. Many Christians are in real peril of failing to fulfil the purpose in their high calling and thereby stand in jeopardy of being disapproved when our Lord will reward His faithful servants. Those who stand the test in that day will be the men and women whose lives brought forth the sweet, pure fruit of the engrafted Word.

Oh, beloved brother, what will the harvest be when we all stand before the Judgment Seat of Christ? Are we taking advantage of every available moment to read and study the Word of God? Do we receive with meekness and all humility its penetrating and purifying truths? The Word thus received is able to save our souls, not from *damnation*, as Guy King so ably states it, but from *damage*. Becoming saved is only the beginning of the Christian life. Regeneration assures the Christian of deliverance from sin's penalty in the life to come, but remember that God's Word provides for the glorious deliverance from sin's power in this present life.

"But be ye doers of the word, and not hearers only, deceiving your own selves" (1:22). Many there are in our churches who read the Bible, respect the Bible, and even reverence the Bible, but do not act upon its teachings. They are merely hearers of the Word. The Bible is the directory of a disciplined and devout life, thus the main business of our lives should be the doing of the Word. Christians should be known as men and women who are doers of God's Word. Whether at business, at home, at school, or at play, it should be said of each one of us that "he is a doer of the Word."

If we suppose ourselves to be religious, or even spiritual because we are familiar with certain Bible truths, or because we are at the hour of preaching, James says that we deceive our own selves. Such self-deception and delusion are common, but it ought not to be so. Life for the Christian must be a continued process of doing what the Bible says; but if we listen to it and do not live it, we cheat and defraud ourselves. Our Lord said that the wise man is the one who hears and does His sayings, while the foolish man is the man who hears them and does them not (Matt. 7:24-27). Why be a fool?

He who merely hears the Word, failing to do it, is like a man beholding his natural face in a mirror (1:23). His "natural face" is the face with which he was born. The purpose of a mirror is to reflect what is imaged in it. The mirror of God's Word is a perfect reflector; it reveals the heart with which we were born. Thank God, His Word does not merely show us up; it will also clean us up. "Wherewithal shall a young man cleanse his way? by taking heed thereto according to Thy Word" (Psalm 119:9).

Beloved, make wise use of your Bible. Do not be guilty of a hasty glance at God's Word, only to turn away forgetting what you saw. Improve your spiritual appearance. The next time you look into the mirror of God's Word, make certain that the stain or blemish you saw when you looked into it at first has been confessed and cleansed. The man who is not a hearer who *forgets,* but a hearer who *does* the Word, "this man shall be blessed in his deed" (1:25). Be an observant and obedient reader and hearer of divine truth. Always take a careful, scrutinizing view of yourself in God's sacred Mirror and beware lest you be a superficial, disobedient reader of your Bible. "If ye know these things, happy are ye if ye do them" (John 13:17). And "to him that knoweth to do good, and doeth it not, to him it is sin" (James 4:17).

As we have stated before, James is quite practical. He is not concerned merely with what a man believes, but how that man behaves. In his desire to impress upon his readers the importance of being doers of the Word and not hearers only, the Apostle sets forth another test whereby the "hearers only" may be sifted from the "doers."

"If any man among you seem to be religious, and bridleth not his tongue, but deceiveth his own heart, this man's religion is vain" (1:26). Look first with me at the words *"religious"* and *"religion."* These words are seldom found in the Bible, not at all in the Old Testament and only five times in the New. The word "religion," used by James here only once and by Luke once in recording Paul's testimony (Acts 26:5), carries the idea of outward religious service. There are those who hear the Word of God and who seem to conform to certain outward forms of ceremony, but who are not saved. Many so-called religions in the world claim earnest, zealous followers, but neither the movements nor their followers can be called Christian merely because they conform to certain outward forms of ritual. Christianity and religion are far from being identical.

But here James is addressing professing Christians, those among the brethren who seem to be religious. Satan sows tares among the wheat and mixes the sheep with the goats so that there are counterfeits among the real. The Pharisees were scrupulous in observing religious rites and ceremonies such as praying, fasting, tithing, and attending church; but the Pharisee's religion was a vain delusion. Such counterfeits creep into many local churches today. They sit with the brethren, sing with the brethren, give with the brethren, and listen to God's Word, but they have never received the Lord Jesus Christ as Saviour. Let my hearers beware! Such a possibility is very real.

Let no man boast about his religion if he "bridleth not his tongue." Space is not lacking in this Epistle when it comes to the subject of the unbridled tongue. It is treated rather fully in Chapter Three. The Scriptures throughout deal thoroughly with this. The religion of many professing Christians has the appearance of genuineness: it appears real but is empty. The Word tells us that out of the abundance of the heart the mouth speaketh. We may not be able to discern the condition of a tree by its roots, but we can come to some conclusions when we examine its fruits. A true test of a man's religion is not his ability to speak his mind, but rather his ability to bridle his tongue. The ability to hold the tongue is one form of self-control, for "if any man offend not in word, the same is a perfect man, and able also to bridle the whole body" (3:2)! Elsewhere the Psalmist says: "I said, I will take heed to my ways, that I sin not with my tongue: I will keep my mouth with a bridle, while the wicked is before me" (Psalm 39:1).

We judge whether a man is real merely by his walk; James says that we are judged also by our talk. A man has but a seeming religion when his tongue is dirty. The Bible is unmistakably clear on this. "Let no corrupt communication proceed out of your mouth, but that which is good to the use of edifying, that it may minister grace unto the hearers" (Eph. 4:29). The sin of speaking rotten, filthy words unfit for use, destroys instead of builds up. The Christian with a foul mouth never promotes the growth of the Body of Christ. If the heart of a man has been cleansed by the blood of Jesus Christ, the words of that man will be clean. If your speech is corrupt, you may *think* you are a Christian; but the Apostle says by the Holy Spirit that you are deceiving your own heart.

A man has but a seeming religion if he has a lying tongue. "Wherefore putting away lying, speak every man truth with his neighbour: for we are members one of another" (Eph. 4:25). Any conscious, intentional falsehood is a word spoken with the intention of deceiving. The devil is a liar and the originator of the lie (John 8:44), and our Lord insisted that all liars have Satan as their father. Satan is to be cast into the lake of fire (Rev. 20:10), and so "all liars shall have their part in the lake which burneth with fire and brimstone" (Rev. 21:8). No man can be called a saved liar. If he is saved at all, he has been saved from lying. "Lie not one to another, seeing that ye have put off the old man with his deeds" (Col. 3:9). The person with the unbridled tongue is not a doer of the Word.

A gossiper has only a seeming religion. Are we guilty of idle talk, spreading groundless rumors, telling scandalous stories we have heard, revealing half-confidential information, or of criticizing someone? James says: "This man's religion is vain." The person with an unbridled tongue has a counterfeit religion that is empty and useless. ". . . Therefore let thy words be few . . ." (Eccl. 5:2). Pray as did David: "Set a watch, O Lord, before my mouth; keep the door of my lips" (Psalm 141:3).

Another test of faith is charity. Now not all charitable persons are saved. Many philanthropic and munificent persons have never received the Lord Jesus Christ as Saviour; but certainly every true child of God will exercise loving care toward orphans, widows, poor, and needy persons. The Apostle John wrote: "But whoso hath this world's good, and seeth his brother have need, and shutteth up his bowels of compassion from him, how dwelleth the love of God in him? My little children, let us not love in word, neither in tongue; but in deed and in truth" (1 John 3:17, 18). Christian love manifests itself both in "tongue" and "deed." James and John agree.

Care for those who need our love and pity is one expression of a pure and undefiled religion. The word "visit" suggests the idea "to care for," "to look after," as when "God hath visited His people" (Luke 1:68; 7:16). Any number of Bible-believing organizations are set for the defense of the faith. There is a greater need for more who are set for the defense of the life, who will insist upon the practical demonstration of the love we preach. We need more Christians who will engage themselves in active Bible philanthropy and thereby assist those in need of temporal or spiritual help.

Men have always believed in the power of possessions, especially money, but no man of wealth can advance himself toward the kingdom of God by his much giving. Many philanthropists will doubtless be in hell. But the principle in our test is that here is something every Christian ought to do. My Christian brothers and sisters, some of you have time for social visits with your special friends, for recreation and entertainment in one form or another; but too few take time to take the blessings of the Gospel to those in need.

We conclude our study of Chapter One with the third test of genuine faith. The doer of the Word will "keep himself unspotted from the world." Do not be disturbed by the words *keep himself*. It is true that the security of the believer, insofar as his salvation is concerned, depends upon God and not man. God assumes His responsibility in *keeping* that which we have committed unto Him against that day (2 Tim. 1:12), but believers are responsible to keep themselves unspotted from the world.

The Bible exhorts: "Keep thyself pure" (1 Tim. 5:22). The present world system is "evil" (Gal. 1:4), and Christians are exhorted neither to be conformed to it (Rom. 12:2) nor to love it (1 John 2:15). True, we are in a dirty world, but we are to keep ourselves unspotted while we pass through. The maxims of the world are opposed to the precepts of God's Word; therefore to conform to the world is to walk in disobedience to the Lord. The Christian has but one choice: he must have no fellowship with the unfruitful works of darkness, but rather reprove them (Eph. 5:11).

My God, my Father, while I stray
Far from my home, on life's rough way,
Oh, teach me from my heart to say,
    "Thy will be done!"

What though in lonely grief I sigh
For friends beloved, no longer nigh,
Submissive still would I reply,
    "Thy will be done!"

Let but my fainting heart be blest,
With Thy sweet Spirit for its guest,
My God, to Thee I leave the rest:
    "Thy will be done!"

Renew my will from day to day:
Blend it with Thine; and take away
All now that makes it hard to say,
    "Thy will be done!"

Then when on earth I breathe no more
The prayer oft mixed with tears before,
I'll sing upon a happier shore,
    "Thy will be done!"

PARTIALITY THROUGH
POOR PERSPECTIVE

James 2:1-4

1. My brethren, have not the faith of our Lord Jesus Christ, the Lord of glory, with respect of persons.

2. For if there come unto your assembly a man with a gold ring, in goodly apparel, and there come in also a poor man in vile raiment;

3. And ye have respect to him that weareth the gay clothing, and say unto him, Sit thou here in a good place; and say to the poor, Stand thou there, or sit here under my footstool:

4. Are ye not then partial in yourselves, and are become judges of evil thoughts?

James is the Epistle of right living. The stress that the Apostle places upon works, however, is not apart from faith but is rather the evidence and fruit of faith. The believer is justified by faith, but he is bound to obedience and good works by what the Bible teaches. James treats faithfully of eternal life, but he does not neglect the external life. In this we servants of the Lord are sometimes weak. True, what a man believes is important, but how he behaves is equally important. A congregation must be taught sound doctrine, but it must be instructed in sacred duty as well.

Chapter Two continues in the vein of practical Christian living. The subject in the verses before us is seldom treated in our local churches. Frankly, I cannot recall ever having heard a sermon against the sin of holding respect of persons on the ground of what a man possesses. Showing partiality to the rich man is here condemned as a sin, and the guilty person is convicted by God's law as being a transgressor. The Christian's attitude toward the rich and the poor is here set forth as a test of faith.

"My brethren, have not the faith of our Lord Jesus Christ, the Lord of glory, with respect of persons" (2:1). This is the fourth time the writer calls his readers "brethren." I find nothing superfluous in this repetition. The brotherhood of believers in Jesus Christ is a glorious one, and we can do with more of heaven's language among brethren. Let us rescue the language of the Bible from the camp of the enemy; we hear much of brotherhood in labor unions and secret societies, but far too little among the children of God.

Apparently, a sin common among brethren today; namely, holding respect for the outward appearance of persons, had crept into the assemblies in the early Church. James is not disapproving honor paid to the rich, but is condemning such action when it is done in such a way as to despise the poor. The "brethren" had professed faith in the Lord Jesus Christ, but such a profession is incompatible with selfish favoritism and covetous partiality.

The appeal of James directs our thought to the person of our Lord Jesus Christ who is the Lord of glory yet never a respecter of persons. There never was a time when glory was completely detached from our blessed Lord. He possessed glory co-equal with that of the Father (Eph. 1:17) and of the Holy Spirit (1 Peter 4:14) in eternity past (John 17:5). In His Incarnation this glory was in evidence, for John wrote: "And the Word was made flesh, and dwelt among us, (and we beheld His glory, the glory as of the only begotten of the Father,) full of grace and truth" (John 1:14). When He comes to earth again it will be in glory, for "they shall see the Son of man coming in the clouds of heaven with power and great glory" (Matt. 24:30). However, with all the glory of Deity attached to the person of Jesus Christ in His past, His present, and His future, at no time did He show Himself to be a "respecter of persons" (Matt. 22:16; Luke 20:21). Our Lord's glory is from everlasting to everlasting, but never once during His earthly ministry did He favor one man over another on the basis of wealth, class, or social distinction. As part of God's household through faith in the Lord Jesus Christ, let us treat God's children equally.

An illustration follows in verses 2 and 3. We cannot be certain whether James actually saw in the assembly at Jerusalem what he relates here or if this is a supposition. Certainly it might well have happened, for Jews tend to worship wealth. In some synagogues, the rich and the rabbis were favored with the chief seats. Our Lord rebuked the Scribes and Pharisees, for, said He: They "love the uppermost rooms at feasts, and the chief seats in the synagogues" (Matt. 23:6). They, too, were known by the clothing they wore and their desire to be saluted in public (Mark 12:38, 39). But such a worldly spirit ought never to creep into the assembly of brethren in Christ.

Here come two men into the worship service. Jewelry and expensive clothing bespeak the first man's wealth. He is greeted at the door with respect and is at once ushered to a choice seat. Believing the well-worn slogan that "Clothes make the man," the usher appears to be impressed with outward appearances. No concern is evidenced as to whether this visitor is clothed with the righteousness and humility of Christ or with his own righteousness (which God says is as filthy rags—Isa. 64:6). We are not judging the motives of the rich man, nor are we suggesting that he should have been treated coldly because he was rich. He may have come by his wealth honestly and put in his appearance at the worship service with a humble and contrite heart. We must examine the rest of the illustration in order to know where the sin lay.

The second visitor was "a poor man in vile raiment" whose humiliating appearance was possibly caused by his soiled garments. He was greeted and judged at once by his outward appearance. Not knowing the truth in the slogan that "You can't judge a book by its cover," the same usher who paid deference to the rich man, coolly tells the shabby-looking visitor either to stand in a corner or to sit on the floor by a footstool. No thought is given by the welcoming committee as to whether or not the poor man is clothed in righteousness (Isa. 61:10) or humility (1 Pet. 5:5) or love (Col. 3:14). He is immediately judged by his outward appearance.

No need to argue the point. We must agree that the rich man was honored for his riches and the poor man was despised because of his poverty. Judgment was passed on mere outward appearances. By so doing it is possible that, in honoring riches, evil also might have been extolled; and in despising the poor, righteousness might have been treated with contempt. Herein lay the sin. If the brother in the assembly had no ulterior motive in his treatment of the rich man but merely to show him that he was welcome in the assembly, he certainly sinned in his contrasting treatment of the poor man.

The world's standard of values is far different from God's. The world makes heroes of people of wealth and fame. The Bible everywhere condemns this respect of persons. God is no respecter of persons (Deut. 1:17; 10:17), and if there is any one place on earth where such conduct ought never to be, it is in the assembly of God's children.

Let me speak frankly about this deplorable practice of favoring the rich. Too often such favoritism is prompted by a selfish motive. The names of poor men seldom appear as sponsors, council members, and references in Christian work. Whom are the directors of Christian organizations trying to impress? What gain are they seeking? Neither a man's money nor his fame qualify him to direct the work of the Lord. This is the world's method of judging and this method has no place in Christian service.

When our Lord distributes rewards to His servants, it surely will not be on the basis of any such worldly practice. Peter told the Lord Jesus how poor he became to follow Him. Our Lord pointed ahead to the world to come and said: "But many that are first shall be last; and the last first" (Mark 10:28-31). Peter's statement naturally follows the two incidents immediately preceding it, the first being the rich man who went away, and the second our Lord's comments on riches and the kingdom of God. Then He proceeded to remind Peter, and us, that in the life to come there will be some surprises. If we cater to the rich for anything we hope to get, or if we look with contempt upon the poor merely because he has nothing to contribute, we will be sadly and disappointedly surprised in the day of judgment. Many a poor, unknown saint will be called up higher, and many a rich, prominent man will be made to stand at the end of the line. Matthew tells us that Peter added the words: "What shall we have therefore?" (Matt. 19:27).

How easily the flesh enters into our service for the Lord! James warns his readers not to respect persons on the basis of outward appearances. The one we place first may be last in heaven. It is a heavenly axiom that "The Lord seeth not as man seeth; for man looketh on the outward appearance, but the Lord looketh on the heart" (1 Sam. 16:7). Be not concerned if the wealthy do not rally to the cause of Christ. Only our omnipotent Lord can be depended upon at all times.

It will be well worth our while to read a brief excerpt from a book by V. Raymond Edman, President of Wheaton College: "Someone had memory long enough to remember the gathering in Chicago in 1923 of the world's most successful financiers of that day, and what became of them—

"Present were . . .

"The president of the largest independent steel company

"The president of the largest utility company

"The greatest wheat speculator

"The president of the New York Stock Exchange

"A member of the President's Cabinet

"The greatest 'bear' in Wall Street

"The president of the Bank of International Settlements

"The head of the world's greatest monopoly

"It has been well said that collectively these tycoons controlled more wealth than there was in the U. S. Treasury.

Newspapers and magazines printed their success stories, urged American youth to follow their examples.

"Twenty-five years later. Let's see what happened to these men . . .

"President of the largest steel company—Charles Schwab —lived on borrowed money the last five years of his life. He died 'broke.'

"Greatest wheat speculator—Arthur Cutten—died abroad—insolvent.

"President of the New York Stock Exchange—Richard Whitney—was recently released from Sing Sing.

"The member of the President's Cabinet—Albert Fall—was pardoned from prison so he could die at home.

"The greatest 'bear' in Wall Street—Jesse Livermore—committed suicide.

"President of the Bank of International Settlements—Leon Fraser—committed suicide.

"The head of the world's greatest monopoly—Ivar Krueger—committed suicide.

"Apparently winning is losing if material factors exceed the spiritual and moral, if selfish and sordid ends are pursued for self-promotion or pique, if increase is at the cost of integrity, and if intrigue be the price of preferment; while apparent losing is winning if there is the courage of convictions and adherence to principles of truth and justice."

It is a rebuke to the worldly spirit among Christians when we show respect of persons implying "What do we get out of it?" Our Lord did not favor the rich. Read again the account of the rich man and Lazarus in Luke 16:19-31. The rich man wore gold rings and goodly apparel in this life, while poor Lazarus was dressed in vile raiment, friendless and hungry. Then one day death came to both. While the minister eulogized the greatness of the rich man, the deceased had dropped his goodly apparel and was at that very moment in hell, so poor he begged for a drop of water. But the poor man in vile raiment despised among the assemblies on earth, at that same moment enjoyed the riches and blessings as an heir of God. Yes, in the life to come, many that are first now shall be last then; and the last shall be first.

James already has taught us that the poor brother in this world's wealth is rich in Christ, and the rich brother is blessed as he is made low (1:9-11). How foolish then to judge a man worthy of praise and prominence, or to condemn a man, by outward circumstances. The practice is not only unreasonable; it is also sinful. How superficial for one who claims to be a servant of Jesus Christ to indulge in such a practice! Fear not to offend the rich nor fail to offer aid to the poor.

When our Lord came to earth to minister, He came as a poor man; when He chose servants, He chose men for the most part poor in this world's goods. He was rich, but for our sakes He became poor (2 Cor. 8:9). The earth and all of its wealth were His, but He neither claimed nor used it for Himself during His earthly sojourn. He said that He was anointed to preach to the poor (Luke 4:18). He said: "When thou makest a feast, call the poor . . ." (Luke 14:13), "distribute unto the poor" (Luke 18:22). He tested the rich man by telling him: "Sell that thou hast, and give to the poor" (Matt. 19:21). The Saviour of men never sought the praises of men, certainly not of the rich. He ministered alike to all. When he called men to serve, He did not choose them because they were financially and socially prominent. For the most part His disciples were insignificantly small in the eyes of the world, but they were willing to leave all and follow Him.

Who speaks with authority in the average church today? Who determines most decisions in a business meeting? Who has the most to say in calling a pastor? Let my reader answer truthfully and he must admit they are those who possess the most prestige.

Luke looked in on a church service attended by the Lord Jesus. This is what he wrote: "And he looked up, and saw the rich men casting their gifts into the treasury. And he saw also a certain poor widow casting in thither two mites. And he said, Of a truth I say unto you, that this poor widow hath cast in more than they all: For all these have of their abundance cast in unto the offerings of God: but she of her penury hath cast in all the living that she had" (Luke 21:1-4). Judging from outward appearances most church groups would favor the rich men casting their gifts into the treasury. But the Lord did not judge them for the amount of money they gave, rather did He judge them for the measure and motive of their giving. In the eyes of the world the poor widow's giving was meager, while the giving of the rich men was much. In the eyes of Him who knows the hearts of all, their offerings were comparatively worthless, while she gave more than they all.

The Lord of glory looks at the degree of self-denial in giving. He was unmoved by the contributions of the rich, for He knew that they made no sacrifice in their giving. Their gifts given out of the abundance of their possessions were, comparatively speaking, trifling. It cost them nothing to bring their offering. The poor widow cast in more than they *all* because she cast in her *all*. How different our Lord's measuring standards are from those of men!

Let the short-sighted pastors and officials who bow to the rich take note. "Are ye not then partial in yourselves, and are become judges of evil thoughts?" (James 2:4). All such have poor discernment and make the wrong kind of distinction. Like the unjust judge in Luke 18:6, they too are judges of injustice. When looking for men to occupy the chair of leadership in the assembly, "look ye out among you . . . men of honest report, full of the Holy Ghost and wisdom, whom we may appoint over this business" (Acts 6:3).

Take time to be holy, speak oft with thy Lord;
Abide in Him always, and feed on His Word.
Make friends of God's children; help those who are weak;
Forgetting in nothing His blessing to seek.

Take time to be holy, the world rushes on;
Spend much time in secret with Jesus alone—
By looking to Jesus, like Him thou shalt be;
Thy friends in thy conduct His likeness shall see.

Take time to be holy, let Him be thy Guide;
And run not before Him, whatever betide;
In joy or in sorrow still follow thy Lord,
And looking to Jesus, still trust in His Word.

Take time to be holy, be calm in thy soul;
Each thought and each temper beneath His control;
Thus led by His Spirit to fountains of love,
Thou soon shalt be fitted for service above.

REPUDIATION THROUGH
DIVINE REASON

James 2:5-7

5. Hearken, my beloved brethren, Hath not God chosen the poor of this world rich in faith, and heirs of the kingdom which he hath promised to them that love him?

6. But ye have despised the poor. Do not rich men oppress you, and draw you before the judgment seats? Do not they blaspheme that worthy name by the which ye are called?

The closer attention the student gives to this neglected Epistle, the more impressed he must become with its practical claims upon his life. The Holy Spirit in this short letter minutely examines subjects elsewhere merely mentioned. Keep in mind the fact that James does not differ with any other writer of Scripture. The Bible has but one Author, and any contradiction or inconsistency would cast aspersion upon God's character and rule out the inerrancy of the message. Do not allow James's emphasis upon *doing* suggest any false idea of lack of harmony between works and faith. The two ideas are not inharmonious; rather they are complementary. Response to doctrine by believing must be followed by responsibility to duty by behaving.

The Apostle has been telling us that faith in our Lord Jesus Christ will result in good works, one of which is the Christian's impartiality. One who professes faith in the Lord Jesus Christ, and at the same time despises the poor, does not possess a true faith that works. The fault of these Christians lies in their reasoning. James now proceeds to repudiate such reasoning by contrasting it with God's.

"Hearken, my beloved brethren, Hath not God chosen the poor of this world rich in faith, and heirs of the kingdom which He hath promised to them that love him?" (verse 5). Since God chooses the poor, by what line of reasoning do we despise them? Our Lord, while here upon earth, did not call the rich to surround Him. He filled the ranks of His army with men who were rich in faith, but not necessarily rich in this world's goods. The haughty Pharisees and rulers of the synagogues would not believe on Him (John 7:48), but the working class followed Him gladly. While our Lord never turned away anyone because he was rich, Jesus began His ministry with a band of men of the poorer class. Although His grace is poured out upon all men (Titus 2:11), apparently the rich were more difficult to deal with than were the poor. God does not choose a man because he is poor, for He places no premium on poverty; but He does choose him because He finds in some poor people a life that is usable in spite of poverty. James, by the Holy Spirit, seeks our special attention on this matter. He says: "Hearken, my beloved brethren." "Listen, pay attention to what God has to say."

Is it a strange thing to you that our Lord imposed poverty upon Himself during His earthly sojourn? His birthplace was a borrowed manger. He said: "Foxes have holes, and birds of the air have nests; but the Son of man hath not where to lay his head" (Luke 9:58). He sought no gain for Himself, and any miracle He ever performed was never done selfishly in His own interest. He needed money to pay taxes and performed a miracle to get it (Matt. 17:27), but He did so only in order that He might render unto Caesar those things that were Caesar's (Luke 20:25; Rom. 13:7). No doubt there are fine rich people who had no choice in their status in life.

The wealth or poverty of our parents is beyond our control, but our Lord had the power of choice. Instead of selecting a woman of riches for His mother, He chose a poor peasant woman. When He lay down His life, His body was placed in a tomb— borrowed from His follower.

Tying in with our subject is an important passage from the pen of the Apostle Paul. "For ye see your calling, brethren, how that not many wise men after the flesh, not many mighty, not many noble, are called: But God hath chosen the foolish things of the world to confound the wise; and God hath chosen the weak things of the world to confound the things which are mighty; And base things of the world, and things which are despised, hath God chosen, yea, and things which are not, to bring to nought things that are: That no flesh should glory in His presence" (1 Cor. 1:26-29). Here is the class of men in whose lives the gospel is more effectively laid hold of. God is not looking necessarily for men with natural attainment, which is what Paul means by the expression "after the flesh." God chooses the "foolish things" (as the world looks upon fools), thereby keeping the glory from the individual. There is always that natural tendency in man that causes him to render his service independent of God and satisfying to himself. A man, of no repute in the opinion of the world, is a sharper tool in God's hands when he fully yields to the Lord than is the influential, wealthy, educated one who because of his pride never bends.

Now the Bible does not suggest that there are not *any* rich people enlisted in God's service, but it does state that there are not *many.* Lady Huntingdon, an English noblewoman, is reported to have said that her calling of God to serve Him depended upon the one letter "m." God did not say "not any" noble, but He did say "not many" noble are called. It appears that Matthew was one of the "not many" class (Matt. 9:9).

In Corinth, as in many churches today, there was that evil tendency to glory in men (1 Cor. 3:3, 21). When a man glories in his own abilities or attainments or achievements, he substitutes self for God. The world bases its progress on power and prestige, but no man can by his own honor and reputation among men offer any solution to world problems nor influence another to God.

History and prophecy both show that the final solution to the ills of this world always rests with humble men, meek men, men poor in spirit but rich in faith toward God and our Lord Jesus Christ. A millionaire or a philosopher may walk out upon the stage of world events, play his role, offer his talent and philosophies and leave the world in spiritual bankruptcy. Send a man —any man, a poor man, an uneducated man—out upon the stage of world events, and let that man declare the gospel of Jesus Christ in the demonstration and power of the Holy Spirit, and lives will be changed with none but God honestly receiving the glory.

Have you ever listened to presiding officers introduce a preacher to an audience? Far beyond the bounds of platform decorum and common courtesy, men laud other men so highly that God is relegated to almost oblivion. This is a curse upon church life today. It caused division in the church at Corinth, and it continues to do the same today.

This, then, is why God chooses those who are poor in this world but who are rich in faith. He wants no man to boast in himself. We may appoint Scribes and Pharisees, but Christ calls publicans and sinners, for often the instruments the world considers foolish are the very things God uses. Though possible to be rich in this world and also rich in faith toward Jesus Christ, the number is few, for the man with wealth and power is in danger of "supposing that gain is godliness" (1 Tim. 6:5).

The Roman Catholic Church is a wealthy institution, many of its followers looking upon that power as godliness. To the church or individual that says: "I am rich, and increased with goods, and have need of nothing," God replies: "[Thou] knowest not that thou art wretched, miserable and poor . . ." (Rev. 3:17). Though a man have no worldly possessions, if he is rich in faith toward Jesus Christ, he can say with Paul: "as having nothing, and yet possessing all things" (2 Cor. 6:10). Our Lord said: "Lay not up for yourselves treasures upon earth, where moth and rust doth corrupt, and where thieves break through and steal: But lay up for yourselves treasures in heaven, where neither moth nor rust doth corrupt, and where thieves do not break through nor steal" (Matt. 6:19, 20). True riches are not deposited in vaults but are laid up in heaven.

Any man who is "poor in spirit," who recognizes the fact

that he has no spiritual assets, that he is spiritually emptied—emptied of self-righteousness and self-confidence—is one whom God can use. There is no virtue in financial poverty, but there is real virtue in the self-abasement that confesses, "I am nothing, I have nothing, and I can do nothing." Let a rich man come thus to God and God will save and use that man. In fact, it is only the humbled He *can* use in His service.

Men who love money more than they love God will lose all in the end, as did the certain rich man in our Lord's parable (Luke 12:16-21). Contrariwise, those who turn to Christ, putting Him first in their hearts, suddenly become generous toward God and man. Zacchaeus was a rich man. When Christ came into his life, he said: "Behold, Lord, the half of my goods I give to the poor; and if I have taken any thing from any man by false accusation, I restore him fourfold" (Luke 19:8). Zacchaeus was a rich man who became poor in spirit. I feel certain that James might have welcomed him as a likely candidate to serve on the official board in the assembly at Jerusalem. A leader in God's work is "not given to filthy lucre; But a lover of hospitality . . ." (Titus 1:7, 8).

Apparently there were some rich men who, in James's day, despised the poor, oppressed them, and even brought them into court (2:6). It seems to this writer that there always has been a tendency for the rich to oppress the poor. Quite recently a woman in our assembly told me of a man and wife whose furniture and clothing were to be sold at a sheriff's sale. I went to that little home at once and learned the following. The husband had passed through a prolonged illness prohibiting his going to work. During his illness his wife had no income whatever. Gradually their meager savings were spent on food, rent, and doctor's bills. Then the woman purchased food on credit and became in arrears in rent payments. After awhile, her landlord and the store owner got together, went to a sheriff, and swore out a warrant for her arrest. Both of her creditors were wealthy men, the landlord being vice-president of our town's largest bank, owner of several

properties, and an elder in a Protestant church. These two creditors are like those rich men of whom James speaks in verse six.
Even some poor, after they become rich, have been known to be
no better than these despisers and oppressors.

"Do not they blaspheme that worthy name by the which ye
are called?" (2:7). Yes, they do! And our Lord tells us exactly
how. There is a proverb that says: "He that oppresseth the poor
reproacheth his Maker: but he that honoureth Him hath mercy
on the poor" (Proverbs 14:31). Since God, who is perfect in
wisdom, permits some to do with little of this world's goods, while
others have an abundance over and above their needs, we dis-
honor Him when we deal severely with the poor. He made both
rich and poor. On what ground then can a Christian fail to show
kindness and sympathy toward those in poverty? Such actions
and attitudes have no Scripture to support them. It is dishonor-
able to the teaching of Christ and thereby brings reproach upon
His Name. Remember, now, that the question before us is not
one of favoring the poor and ignoring the rich. The point is that
when a man has real faith in the Lord Jesus Christ, he will show
equal love and sympathy toward both.

When our Lord comes back to earth to set up His kingdom, He
shall gather all nations before Him for judgment (Matt. 25:31-
46). This judgment is not the judgment of the great white throne
of Revelation, chapter 20, but of the living nations. The judgment
of the great white throne is after the millennium; this is before
the millennium. He will say to the sheep on His right hand: "For
I was an hungred, and ye gave me meat: I was thirsty, and ye
gave me drink: I was a stranger, and ye took me in: Naked, and
ye clothed me: I was sick, and ye visited me: I was in prison, and
ye came unto me" (verses 35-36). We are not to suppose here
that the salvation of the sheep will be on the ground of their good
works, but by their works they will have proved the genuineness
of their faith.

So genuine is the love of the Christian that he is not even
conscious of having ministered to his Lord, so he asks: "When

saw we thee an hungred, and fed thee? or thirsty, and gave thee drink? When saw we thee a stranger, and took thee in? or naked, and clothed thee? Or when saw we thee sick, or in prison, and came unto thee?" (verses 37-39).

Then shall he answer them: "Inasmuch as ye have done it unto one of the least of these my brethren, ye have done it unto Me" (verse 40).

Notice please how our Lord Jesus Christ recognizes anything done for others in His Name as done unto Himself. He said elsewhere: "And whosoever shall give to drink unto one of these little ones a cup of cold water only in the name of a disciple, verily I say unto you, he shall in no wise lose his reward" (Matt. 10:42).

Then He turns to speak to those on His left hand and says: "Depart from me, ye cursed, into everlasting fire, prepared for the devil and his angels: For I was an hungred, and ye gave me no meat: I was thirsty, and ye gave me no drink: I was a stranger, and ye took me not in: naked, and ye clothed me not: sick, and in prison, and ye visited me not" (verses 41-43). We are not to suppose here that these were condemned merely because they did no good works, but by refusing to do good they proved their lack of faith, for, as James shows us later in this chapter, "Faith without works is dead" (James 2:17, 20).

Then the accused plead their cause on the ground of ignorance, saying: "Lord, when saw we thee an hungred, or athirst, or a stranger, or naked, or sick, or in prison, and did not minister unto thee?" (verse 44).

To their utter dismay and hopelessness they will hear Him say: "Inasmuch as ye did it not to one of the least of these, ye did it not to Me" (verse 45). In failing to be merciful to the poor they showed contempt for the Lord of glory who became poor in order that poor lost sinners might receive the blessings of heaven.

The lesson in these verses finds application in all who name His Name. There are those all about us who need Christ's love and care; and while the inheritance of the church is far higher than that meted out to the living nations in this Scripture when Christ comes in glory, any lack of love on the part of believers will mean loss of reward at the Judgment Seat of Christ.

There is a principle in James 2:7 that bears a close relationship to that taught by our Lord in Matthew 25:31-46. It is the principle of charity toward all and partiality toward none. When a professing Christian is uncharitable toward any man, he does despite to the Name of Jesus Christ who loves all men.

Free from the law, oh, happy condition!
Jesus hath bled, and there is remission!
Cursed by the law, and bruised by the fall,
Grace hath redeemed us once for all.

Now are we free—there's no condemnation,
Jesus provides a perfect salvation;
"Come unto Me,"—oh, hear His sweet call,
Come, and He saves us once for all.

Children of God! oh, glorious calling!
Surely His grace will keep us from falling;
Passing from death to life at His call,
Blessed salvation, once for all.

Once for all, O sinner, receive it;
Once for all, O brother, believe it;
Cling to the Cross, the burden will fall;
Christ hath redeemed us once for all.

JUDGMENT THROUGH
DIVINE LAW

James 2:8-9

8. If ye fulfil the royal law according to the scripture, Thou shalt love thy neighbour as thyself, ye do well:

9. But if ye have respect to persons, ye commit sin, and are convinced of the law as transgressors.

The Apostle has not finished with the subject with which this chapter began. He is still dealing with a sin God hates: namely, respect of persons, the sin of being favorable toward the rich while despising the poor. In this chapter we shall take up a study of those verses which show plainly that any wrong treatment of the poor is a violation of God's law; therefore those Christians who were guilty must be made to see that they are lawbreakers. I fear that we are inclined to treat this fault only as unreasonable, whereas the Scripture labels it emphatically as downright sinful.

For all Christians one law controls our treatment of all men. James calls this law "the royal law according to the scripture" (2:8). It may be referred to as "royal" because it is a "kingly" or "sovereign" law, having its origin in the courts of heaven. It is the law of *love*, having been exemplified in the life of Jesus Christ who is the King of kings. It is the law of Christ's kingdom and as such controls the conduct of His subjects. All true believers are of the "royal priesthood" (1 Peter 2:9) and must therefore be guided by this law.

This law that controls our attitude toward all men is said to be "according to the scripture." James, like all true servants of Jesus Christ, believed in the inspiration and infallibility of the Holy Scriptures. To them he appeals as his authority. It is our

purpose here to examine the Scriptures that we might learn more
of this divine rule of life to keep it with integrity of heart.

The law follows: "Thou shalt love thy neighbour as thyself."
The significance of an improper respect of persons represents a
violation of the basic and fundamental law of the Kingdom of
God, namely, the law of love. In all of His teaching ministry,
our Lord stressed the crucial importance of this law. The believer's relationship to God and to his fellowman may be
summed up in one sweeping statement given by Jesus Christ
when He said: "Thou shalt love the Lord thy God with all thy
heart, and with all thy soul, and with all thy mind. This is the
first and great commandment. And the second is like unto it,
Thou shalt love thy neighbour as thyself. On these two commandments hang all the law and the prophets" (Matt. 22:37-40). This
He gave in answer to the question of the Pharisees, "Master,
which is the greatest commandment in the law?" You can see at
once that James is quoting a statement of our Lord.

Perhaps your enquiring mind asks the question that a lawyer
once asked of Christ: "And who is my neighbour?" (Luke
10:29). It was in answer to this question that our Lord told that
beautiful and well-known story of the Good Samaritan. A certain
man, while taking a journey from Jerusalem to Jericho, was
robbed and beaten by thieves. A priest passing by, looked at the
helpless victim lying upon the ground, completely ignoring him.
A Levite came along and did likewise. Now mark you, these two
men who offered no help to the badly beaten victim were very
religious. Soon a certain Samaritan passing that way saw the man
and had compassion on him. The Samaritan bound up his wounds,
took him to an inn, and paid the innkeeper for the care of the
man. Now, asked Jesus, "Which . . . was neighbour unto him
that fell among the thieves?"

Quickly the discerning lawyer gave Him the only reply. He
said: "He that shewed mercy on him." "Then said Jesus unto
him, Go, and do thou likewise" (Luke 10:25-37). I feel certain that the answer of the Lord Jesus smote that man's con-

science and made him realize he never fully met the requirements of the law of God. Our neighbor is not merely one who lives nearby but one who needs our help as well as one who helps our need. God's law of love is not limited by creed, color, financial status or social standing; it reaches out to all the needy everywhere. Those Christians to whom James wrote had in their group some who looked upon the rich man as their neighbor, but not the poor man. In so doing they were violating God's royal law of love.

The priest and the Levite had the same knowledge of the unfortunate traveler's need and the same opportunity to assist as the Samaritan; yet neither of them showed any love whatever. The reason why is not given. Possibly they were proud, or perhaps they saw that the beaten man had nothing to pay. One thing is certain: each failed to see the claim of the needy upon him and his debt of love to that need.

Love finds and makes neighbors of those who need our love. This is practical Christianity at its best, and failure here is not Christianity at all, "for he that loveth not his brother whom he hath seen, how can he love God whom he hath not seen?" (1 John 4:20). This inspired statement of the Apostle John leads us back to our Lord's answer to the question, "Master, which is the great commandment in the law?" In His reply Jesus said that a man must love God with all his heart, soul, and mind, and his neighbor as himself. Now there are those who would tell us they love God while failing to show love to their needy fellowmen. Such is not true! Love for God and none for man are diametrically opposite principles, so far removed the one from the other that God says: "If a man say, I love God, and hateth his brother, he is a liar" (1 John 4:20).

Let every professing believer beware! Saying that we love God does not make it so. I know of no point of Christian teaching in which we can deceive ourselves as easily as in this. It is much easier to say that we love God than it is to show love, yet love to our fellowman is one of the fruits of divine love. When we are born again, "the love of God is shed abroad in our hearts by the Holy Ghost which is given unto us" (Rom. 5:5), and the first known fruit of the Spirit in the believer is "love" (Gal. 5:22). The Christian will love as God loved him, with the very same sort of love.

God saw me in my need and His love moved toward me to meet that need. "God commendeth His love toward us, in that, while we were yet sinners, Christ died for us" (Rom. 5:8). If I have received that love, it must go forth through me to others in their need. My love must be what God's love is, no idle expression of sentiment or dreamy piety, but a love that seeks the needy and gives liberally without upbraiding. May I ignore a man because he is poor, shabbily clothed, uneducated? Did God ignore me when I was unfit for heaven? How would it be with me now if God ignored me as I ignore others? I confess it almost makes me tremble at the very thought of it. "This commandment have we from Him, That he who loveth God love his brother also" (1 John 4:21). James is right "according to the Scripture" when he says: "[If] thou shalt love thy neighbour as thyself, ye do well."

The Lord Jesus says: "A new commandment I give unto you, That ye love one another; as I have loved you, that ye also love one another" (John 13:34). Notice that we have here a command, and it is not unreasonable, to be certain. Our Lord is not calling upon an unregenerate man to be charitable or philanthropic. He addresses His own, those indwelt by God Himself, and every one who is born of the Spirit has in him the love of God. Faith, Hope, and Love are three inseparable virtues possessed by every child of God, and these remain when all else fails (1 Cor. 13:13); moreover, "the greatest of these is love." Love remains the outstanding proof of our relationship to God. Every branch of Christendom claims to be the true Church and Christ's only representative on earth; but the supreme test of a church or an individual is love, for Jesus says: "By this shall all men know that ye are My disciples, if ye have love one to another" (John 13:35).

A profession of faith in Christ is empty and vain apart from love. The Apostle John writes: "And this is His commandment, That we should believe on the name of His Son Jesus Christ, and love one another, as He gave us commandment" (1 John 3:23). This verse strikes a blow at those who contend that a man's behavior is not necessarily controlled by what he believes. A man's faith is always basic of his actions. Right living depends upon right believing. True faith is expressed in true love. The command is twofold: believe on Jesus Christ, and love one another. It is the Biblical combination of faith and works. Actually it is one commandment. Love is the outward expression of the inward reality of faith. Nothing we do will please the Father more than to believe on Jesus Christ and love one another.

James adds the words "as thyself" to show the measure, or extent, of love. In other words, I am to show the same interest in the welfare of others as I would show toward myself. Does this sound too exacting? Does it seem unreasonably demanding? Did not our Lord command us to love one another *as He loved us* (John 13:34)? After He repeated this commandment, He added: "Greater love hath no man than this, that a man lay down his life for his friends" (John 15:13). Lay down His life is exactly what He did, for, "having loved His own which were in the world, He loved them unto the end" (John 13:1). That is loving others as thyself. It is the teaching of Scripture throughout. "Bear ye one another's burdens, and so fulfil the law of Christ" (Gal. 6:2). "Hereby perceive we the love of God, because He laid down His life for us: and we ought to lay down our lives for the brethren" (1 John 3:16).

"Look not every man on his own things, but every man also on the things of others" (Phil. 2:4). We should evince such a love for one another that the good of each other is our deepest concern. No Christian should live a self-centered life, that is, looking only after his own interests; but should look after the interests of others as well. Living for self is fleshly, indulgent, selfish. The watchword of our lives should be *others*, esteeming *others* better than ourselves (Phil. 2:3).

Occupation with our "own things" is a great hindrance in any Christian's life. Selfishness may be natural to an unsaved man, but the child of God has been supernaturally born from above, and his seeking must be after those things which are above (Col. 3:1) and not on things on the earth (Col. 3:2). Oh beloved, let us look out for others, and God will look out for us. Our heavenly Father is never debtor to those who fulfil His royal law, and this law applies to every Christian, whether rich or poor.

And now sternly James condemns those who are guilty of lack of love. "You sin," he charges them. "But if ye have respect to persons, ye commit sin, and are convinced of the law as transgressors" (2:9). The context in Chapter Two strikes at those who flatter and pamper the rich while they despise and neglect the poor. In spite of their profession of faith in the Lord Jesus Christ, their hearts were not fixed on laying up treasure in heaven and in the life to come, but on the treasures of this world. For this he could not commend them but only condemn them. Nay, he needed not to condemn them, for in having respect of persons they had committed sin and were convicted already by the law as transgressors.

In the closing words of Chapter One we are exhorted to keep ourselves "unspotted from the world." Here is a form of worldliness if ever there was one. Who is worshiped by the world today? Those who are wealthy, successful; those who have achieved fame in sports, show business, and such. When a Christian falls into the same snare he becomes guilty of idolatry, which is worldly. My Christian brothers and sisters, this is a grave matter. Do not treat it lightly. Through this one offence you fail to meet the requirements of God's law, and by His law you are convicted. Love for all mankind is the law of God's kingdom, the law by which the King Himself came into this world of sin and lived and died. Think of it! God Himself is ruled by His own law of love. And this same law must be the Christian's rule. Exclusiveness, caste, selfishness, all of which show "respect of persons," have no place in the divine economy.

At this point someone may be asking: "Is there no place whatever for social differences?" This writer believes that there is. These differences exist in the very nature and structure of things as seen in man's history. In my ministry as a pastor I have come across many persons who showed no desire to rise above their present level. Others cared nothing for accomplishment or success. But social differences, even though they be of one's own choice, do not give the Christian any license whatever to break God's law. If the differences exist, let there be no cliques, parties, or factions; rather let there be sweetness, sympathy, love, and courtesy at all times and toward all classes. If paying attention to one of the upper class will help him spiritually, by all means do it, but never to the neglect of, or at the expense of one of the lower class. Such respect of persons is not only a breach of good manners: it is a sin. God's law demands equality of treatment for rich and poor. Exercise great care lest you expose yourself to the just judgment of God. This is no trifling matter; it is a serious moral offence.

I hear the Saviour say,
  "Thy strength indeed is small;
Child of weakness, watch and pray,
  Find in Me thine all in all."

Lord, now indeed I find
  Thy power, and Thine alone,
Can change the leper's spots,
  And melt the heart of stone.

For nothing good have I
  Whereby Thy grace to claim—
I'll wash my garments white
  In the blood of Calvary's Lamb.

When from my dying bed
  My ransomed soul shall rise,
Then "Jesus paid it all!"
  Shall rend the vaulted skies.

And when before the Throne
  I stand in Him complete,
I'll lay my trophies down,
  All down at Jesus' feet.

Jesus paid it all—
  All to Him I owe;
Sin had left a crimson stain;
  He washed it white as snow.

GUILTY THROUGH
ONE OFFENCE

James 2:10-13

10. For whosoever shall keep the whole law, and yet offend in one point, he is guilty of all.

11. For he that said, Do not commit adultery, said also, Do not kill. Now if thou commit no adultery, yet if thou kill, thou art become a transgressor of the law.

12. So speak ye, and so do, as they that shall be judged by the law of liberty.

13. For he shall have judgment without mercy, that hath shewed no mercy; and mercy rejoiceth against judgment.

In writing his Epistle, James doubtless anticipated that his readers would be somewhat surprised, and possibly rebellious, over his telling them that the law convicted them as transgressors because they showed respect to persons. I must confess that, in my first casual readings of the Book of James, I too felt that these were hard sayings. If some who have followed me in these messages may be saying the same thing even now, be not hasty in judgment. Remember, James is writing by inspiration of the Holy Spirit, and certainly none of us would dare to find fault with anything God would say to us.

Just how do we violate God's law when we fraternize and socialize with the rich and neglect the poor? We have seen already that love toward God and our fellowmen is the basic structure of the whole law. Now James adds: "For whosoever shall keep the whole law, and yet offend in one point, he is guilty of all" (2:10). This verse does two things: it elucidates the subject, shedding light upon the problem as seen in the question just raised; and it emphasizes the guilt of those who violate the "royal law" of love. James does not mean that sins are equally great in magnitude and in their damaging results. He is saying, however, that the breaking of one commandment does put the offender in the class of transgressors.

Some lessons to be learned from verse 10 follow. First, any violation of any single commandment means that the violator is disobedient to the Lawgiver. The principle of obedience is involved here. Should a child persist in disobeying only one of his father's rules in particular, would that child be classified as a disobedient son? Most assuredly! Moreover, such persistency in disobeying only the one injunction of the father would prove positively that the child was possessed of a disobedient spirit, and the father would be justified in raising a question about all of the son's conduct. It takes but one lie to make a liar, one act of adultery to make an adulterer, one theft to make a thief, one murder to make a murderer, and only one broken law to make a lawbreaker. It takes only one offence to cause me to fall short of the requirements of the Law.

Secondly, verse 10 teaches that the Law of God is a unified whole. Let all who pride themselves in their lawkeeping beware! Nieboer likens the law to a seamless garment that is rent, although torn only in one place. D. L. Moody compared God's law to a chain of ten links suspending a man over a precipice. If all ten links break, the man falls to his doom. If five of the ten links break, the man falls to his doom. And if only one link breaks, the man falls to his doom just the same. Another has likened the law to a circle broken by only one piece being out of place. To violate the law in one point is to be a lawbreaker. Jehovah had said to Israel: "Therefore shall ye observe *all* my statutes, and all my judgments, and do them: I am the Lord" (Lev. 19:37). Now James is not intimating that if a man breaks one commandment in the law he might just as well go ahead and break all the others. But rather, if a man breaks every commandment, or only one commandment, he is a certain kind of person: namely, a lawbreaker.

Recently, a man in our community was apprehended, tried by

a jury, and found guilty of murdering a neighborhood girl. During the course of the trial a number of character witnesses appeared to testify in behalf of the accused man. All the good things about him that the witnesses presented did not move judge or jury when sentence was passed. The prosecuting attorney emphasized the fact that the man was not being tried for any existing goodness in him, nor for the laws he did not break, but for the law he did break. He was found guilty of murder and sentenced to death in the electric chair.

Verse 10 speaks to sinner and saint alike. Let all who are depending upon their good works to save them ponder seriously this verse and the following. "For as many as are of the works of the law are under the curse: for it is written, Cursed is every one that continueth not in all things which are written in the book of the law to do them" (Gal. 3:10). Neither James nor Paul is saying that lawkeeping will save anyone. "Therefore we conclude that a man is justified by faith without the deeds of the law" (Rom. 3:28).

If salvation could come by lawkeeping, then it would not have been necessary for Christ to die on the cross. Christ was the only man who ever kept the law fully, and He died that guilty man might be delivered from the penalty of the law he had broken. "Christ hath redeemed us from the curse of the law, being made a curse for us: for it is written, Cursed is every one that hangeth on a tree" (Gal. 3:13). Nothing can be added to the work of the Lord Jesus Christ at Calvary.

Sinners are under neither law nor works for salvation. We are saved by grace through faith, and that not of ourselves; it is the gift of God (Eph. 2:8). Thank God, the sinner's salvation does not depend upon his law-keeping, for then he never could be saved. If a man could keep all of God's commandments, save one, the violation of that one would make him a violator of divine law and subject to divine punishment.

The Apostle now turns to the One on whose authority the law rests. "For He that said, Do not commit adultery, said also, Do not kill. Now if thou commit no adultery, yet if thou kill, thou art become a transgressor of the law" (2:11). Here James refers to the sixth and seventh commandments of the Decalogue (Exod. 20:13, 14) to illustrate a point: namely, the law in its entirety has but one Author; "All Scripture is given by inspiration of God . . ." (2 Tim. 3:16). Any breach of God's law, in its minutest detail, strikes against the Author. Who is man to choose certain of God's commandments to obey and certain of them to break?

A true child of God will strive at all times to obey his Lord in all His precepts. Some in the assembly in James's day thought that their petty sin of having respect to persons was not really important. They might have excused themselves by saying: "I have not committed adultery," or, "I have not killed any one"; but James could only tell them that even though they refrained from certain sins and committed only one other, they had become transgressors of the law. Since love is the summation of all law, they were violators because they had acted contrary to divine love when they failed to show love to the poor, for God had said: ". . . Thou shalt not respect the person of the poor, nor honour the person of the mighty . . ." (Lev. 19:15).

Look more closely at the thought of divine authority in connection with the law. Every word of the Decalogue that God gave to Moses was supernaturally inscribed by the finger of God (Deut. 9:10). James is telling us that the commandments constitute what God said. Divine law is no mere ordinance of man. The authority behind any law determines the seriousness of the offence. Violation of federal law carries more serious consequences than violation of a city law. Stealing a letter from an office desk would not be as serious an offence, nor would it bring as severe a penalty, as stealing a letter from a government mailbag. The greatest Authority in all the universe is God its creator. He has a law that reads: "Be not deceived; God is not mocked: for whatsoever a man soweth, that shall he also reap" (Gal. 6:7). But our hearts should rejoice in that He, the greatest and most exacting Lawgiver, is also man's greatest Benefactor and only Redeemer. Bless His Name, there is salvation and deliverance for any and all lawbreakers; for "Christ hath redeemed us from the curse of the law, being made a curse for us: for it is written, Cursed is every one that hangeth on a tree" (Gal. 3:13).

Emphatically, no man in this present age will be lost for failing to keep any part of God's law. Every unregenerated man "is condemned already, because he hath not believed in the name of the only begotten Son of God" (John 3:18). By the same token, no man will be saved because he kept any part of God's law. "For by grace are ye saved through faith; and that not of yourselves: it is the gift of God: Not of works, lest any man should boast" (Eph. 2:8, 9).

As James again addresses believers, he adds: "So speak ye, and so do, as they that shall be judged by the law of liberty" (2:12). For the second time the Apostle uses this phrase, "law of liberty" (see 1:25). Just what we are to understand by "the law of liberty," I cannot be certain. Some students of the Bible apply it to the Gospel of our Lord Jesus Christ which sets the believing sinner free from the penalty of a broken law and from the power of sin. This view is conceivable since Jesus said: "And ye shall know the truth, and the truth shall make you free" (John 8:32), and again: "If the Son therefore shall make you free, ye shall be free indeed" (John 8:36). Others make the "law of liberty" to mean the Ten Commandments from whose bondage the believer has been set free. This latter view I find difficult to accept. True, the law is holy (Rom. 7:12) and spiritual (Rom. 7:14), but at no time were the Gentiles under the law.

What, then, can be meant by the "law of liberty"? Ordinarily the law restrains liberty. The two are not usually thought of as having anything in common. Liberty is understood by most to mean freedom from rules, regulations, and restraint. The "law of liberty" is, to them, a paradox, but, then, is not the Christian life a paradox to the natural mind? James has dealt with some of these paradoxes, such as "Patience Through Tribulation" and

"Riches Through Poverty." Could it be that the law of liberty is an inward constraint instead of an outward restraint? We have learned that the royal law, according to the Scriptures, is the law of love. Now if I am truly born again, indwelt by the spirit of God, a partaker of the very nature of God, then it follows that I will be prefectly free to do that which is right, not by restraint, but by constraint. Paul wrote: "For the love of Christ constraineth us . . ." (2 Cor. 5:14). The royal law of love, controlling our lives, causes us to want to reflect the life of our Lord. How dissatisfied we all have been with life on the natural plane of the old unregenerate, selfish life! Many of us had desires to be idealistic, but we witnessed selfishness, disloyalty, and untrustworthiness in ourselves as well as in others. We discovered that we were bound and had not the liberty to do those things that God's laws demanded of men.

Then came the hour of our regeneration. We were born again, made new creatures in Christ, and the love of God was shed abroad in our hearts. We were suddenly conscious of a new Master, a new motive, to drive us, to constrain us. With a glorious and happy freedom we found ourselves reaching out to love as Jesus loved. The royal law had done its work in us. Love, the love of God in Christ, had captured our hearts, mastered us; we willingly and gladly surrendered to it. And why not? His love had redeemed us, set us free from the penalty of a broken law; now His passionate concern for men is ours. Oh wondrous compulsion! There is no longer a struggle to become free from anything, or to do anything. We *are* free. Benevolence and love toward others did not. make us Christians, for then all philanthropists would be Christians. But having recognized that God in love sent Jesus Christ to die for us, and that in His loving us and dying for us we are saved, we are now set free by His all-conquering love to go out into a world of sinners to show forth His love. Is not this the law of liberty?

"So speak ye, and so do, as they that shall be judged by the law of liberty" (2:12). We are informed here that there is a day of judgment for the believer, and that both his words and actions are to be judged in accordance with that law which he received. No Christian ever need fear the great white throne judgment which is for unbelievers only. No child of God can ever be condemned with the wicked (John 5:24; Rom. 8:1), not even for having broken any or all of the Ten Commandments, for we are not under law but under grace (Rom. 6:14). Nevertheless there is a day, yet future, when all Christians must appear before the Judgment Seat of Christ (Rom. 14:10; 2 Cor. 5:10) where our works will be made manifest without disguise. At that day every believer's work shall be tried, and all injustices shall be made right. The believer is not on trial, but his "work" is (1 Cor. 3:13-15).

Can a believer plead mercy at the Judgment Seat of Christ? By no means! God will have the true record of my words and works, and by that record they shall be weighed. Verse 13 is clear on this point. The believer who shows no mercy "shall have judgment without mercy." There is nothing legalistic nor unfair about this judgment. The rewards will be given or withheld, as the case may be, on the ground of divine justice. Some who have been elevated by men to lofty honors here on earth will be dismayed at that day. Our Lord will deal justly with us all. Those Christians who lived selfishly, showing no mercy upon needy men and women, will be shown no mercy when rewards are given. If the royal law of love does not triumph in all our dealings with our fellowmen, we can look for no mercy. James is applying what our Lord taught in Matthew 7:1, 2, namely, "With what measure ye mete, it shall be measured to you again." If we judge others and show no mercy toward them, we ourselves shall be dealt with in judgment without mercy.

Let us remember that "mercy rejoiceth against judgment." This means that mercy triumphs over judgment. If I show mercy to the needy instead of sitting in judgment upon them, I shall triumph in the end at the Judgment Seat of Christ. The Apostle John says that love has boldness in the day of judgment (1 John

4:17). Outward actions show very clearly what a man is at heart now, as well as what his reward will be hereafter. When a Christian shows compassion on others at all times, he looks forward to the judgment with calm confidence. A heart full of mercy has no fear of the day of judgment but rejoices in the face of it.

I came a wanderer, and alone,
  My way was dark as night;
I looked to Thee, O blessed One,
  And then I found the light.

I came with all my doubts and fears,
  No hope but in Thy Word;
And while I gazed upon the blood,
  Thy pardoning voice I heard.

Oh, may the Spirit's power be felt
  In this poor heart of mine,
And make Thy Word my lamp and light,
  My shield and strength divine.

Oh, teach me, Lord, Thy voice to know,
  Amid the surging throng;
Be Thou my hope, my life, my joy,
  My everlasting song.

O Jesus, Saviour, Lamb of God,
  How much I owe to Thee,
For all the wonders of Thy grace,
  And all Thy love to me!

SALVATION THROUGH
THE WORD OF FAITH

James 2:14-20

14. What doth it profit, my brethren, though a man say he hath faith, and have not works? can faith save him?

15. If a brother or sister be naked, and destitute of daily food,

16. And one of you say unto them, Depart in peace, be ye warmed and filled; notwithstanding ye give them not those things which are needful to the body; what doth it profit?

17. Even so faith, if it hath not works, is dead, being alone.

18. Yea, a man may say, Thou hast faith, and I have works: shew me thy faith without thy works, and I will shew thee my faith by my works.

19. Thou believest that there is one God; thou doest well: the devils also believe, and tremble.

20. But wilt thou know, O vain man, that faith without works is dead?

The remaining verses of Chapter Two must be examined with care. It is this section of James that has been up for controversy, and that has made some people feel that here James contradicts Paul. Let me remind you once again that "All Scripture is given by inspiration of God . . ." (2 Tim. 3:16), meaning, of course, that the writings of James and Paul have but one real Author, and the Holy Spirit cannot contradict Himself. Any interpretation of the Word of God which seems to make God contradict Himself is always a failure on man's part to interpret rightly what God has said.

Banish from your minds once for all any semblance of the idea that James repudiates salvation by faith in Christ. He does no such thing. James and Paul must agree on this, as on every other doctrine, since both wrote exactly what the Spirit of God directed them to write. James teaches that "Faith alone saves, but the faith that saves is not alone"; it is always attended by good works.

"What doth it profit, my brethren, though a man say he hath faith, and have not works? can faith save him?" (2:14). This verse, with those that immediately follow, form a strong attack against a dead faith, a faith without works. You will recall that James exhorts to "Be ye doers of the word, and not hearers only, deceiving your own selves" (1:22). Here he is but echoing the teachings of our Lord when He said: "And every one that heareth these sayings of mine, and doeth them not, shall be likened unto a foolish man . . ." (Matt. 7:26). A man may hear the truth and even *say* that he believes, but unless the fruits of living faith are evident in his life, he is not saved at all. The appeal is to be what you say you believe. You call yourself a Christian; then be a Christian.

The reference here is to the man that will "say" he has faith, but his saying so does not make it so. Merely saying that I am a Christian does not make me a Christian. I may make a false pretence of believing something of which I am wholly destitute. Now if I say I have faith, but my life does not correspond to that which I profess, can the faith that I say I have save me? This is what James is asking in the question, "Can faith save him?" The answer is an emphatic "No." For a faith that produces no works cannot save anyone. There is no profit in a man claiming to possess something which he actually does not have.

Possibly these verses before us in James are striking at the very heart of the spiritual and moral weakness in much church life today. Faith to many is giving mental assent to a fact. A man may be asked if he believes that Jesus Christ is the Son of God and the Saviour of the world. He answers positively and affirmatively because he has never believed anything else. He was raised in the midst of orthodoxy. The Bible facts about Jesus Christ being born of a virgin, dying for sinners, and being raised the third day from the dead have always been a part of his thinking; but a head knowledge and mental assent to Christian truth does not make one a Christian. A dead faith is both unproductive and unprofitable. When one has a faith that works, he will show by his life the works of faith. A genuine belief in the truth will produce a genuine behavior of the truth. Some people in our churches are all *profession,* the emphasis being placed on what they "say." Our Lord said: "Not every one that *saith* unto Me, Lord, Lord, shall enter into the kingdom of heaven; but he that *doeth* the will of my Father which is in heaven" (Matt. 7:21). Now James is not asking: "Can faith save?" but "Can faith save *him* who merely says he has faith but who fails to do the will of God?" James says that that man shall not enter into the kingdom of heaven.

True faith necessarily results in fruit after its kind. This principle James is about to illustrate. "If a brother or sister be naked, and destitute of daily food, And one of you say unto them, Depart in peace, be ye warmed and filled; notwithstanding ye give them not those things which are needful to the body; what doth it profit?" (2:15, 16). If a man does not show love toward those in need, he thereby shows that his faith is not a true and living one. Lip service to the principle of Christianity is no proof that one is saved. You may go so far as to pray for those in need, but without corresponding action, your prayers and testimonies constitute hypocrisy in its worst form. What profit is your profession of faith to you, or to anyone else, if you dismiss the needy with prayers and good wishes while you withhold from them the necessities of life? The Apostle John adds his comment to that of James: "But whoso hath this world's good, and seeth his brother have need, and shutteth up his bowels of compassion from him, how dwelleth the love of God in him? My little children, let us not love in word, neither in tongue; but in deed and in truth" (1 John 3:17, 18). Faith is not a matter of words alone, but of words and works. Words that express regret and pity for those in need but are not backed up with good works are hypocritical words. A faith that witnesses suffering and is not stirred to help is worth nothing.

Whenever our Lord said "Depart in peace," those words were no mere pious, fraudulent, well-wishing words, but expressed a benediction. That benediction was accompanied by merciful acts (Luke 7:50; 8:48). The Apostle exhorted: "As we have therefore opportunity, let us do good unto all men, especially unto them who are of the household of faith" (Gal. 6:10).

The present life affords the believer his one opportunity to show forth the fruits of his faith in Jesus Christ. Constantly, we must be bearing the burdens of others and sharing our spiritual and temporal blessings; we are debtors to all men to do them good by word and deed. Let us not relax our efforts in behalf of the unsaved, and let us increase them in behalf of our brethren in Christ. Hold your nice words and sweet sentiments if they are devoid of action, for what do they profit? Do they feed the hungry? Do they restore the erring? Do they comfort the needy? No, in nowise! God has joined together faith and works. Let us never attempt to put them asunder. If you are satisfied with a faith without works, you had better examine yourself to make certain whether or not you have the true and living faith. A faith that is a mere assent to a creed is not worthy of the name.

James proceeds to show just what is wrong with a man's faith which claims to believe in the Lord Jesus Christ and at the same time violates the law of love. He says: "Even so faith, if it hath not works, is dead, being alone" (2:17). Faith in the God of love and in the love of God cannot stand alone. Without works a man's faith is dead. By the same token, without faith a man's works are dead. It is a "dead" faith which says "I believe" and at the same time produces none of the fruits of faith. Such a faith stands alone, having nothing to stand with it nor to substantiate it. It is dead, unproductive, and unprofitable. In the first verse of Chapter Two James tells us that spiritual life has its origin and root in "the faith of our Lord Jesus Christ," but all that follows verse one insists that a certain course of behavior will coincide with such belief.

What might the Apostle mean by faith that is "dead"? There

is a faith unto salvation and a faith that is not unto salvation. Saving faith is more than believing in *God*. There will be many people in hell who were not atheists but believers in God. Saving faith is more than believing in *one* God. Likewise there will be monotheists in hell who were not idolators. The Apostle writes: "Thou believest that there is one God; thou doest well: the devils also believe, and tremble" (2:19). Demons are not atheists. They believe there is a God, and they shudder at the thought of Him. Moreover, they believe in the deity of Christ. On one occasion they said: ". . . What have we to do with thee, Jesus, thou Son of God . . . ?" (Matt. 8:29). Yet for all their belief and confession of Jesus Christ, demons are not saved nor can they ever be. Demons believe and yet remain demons. Even so, unsaved persons can believe and remain unsaved. The one difference between demons and men is that men can be saved. But in order to be saved, one must have saving faith.

Simon the sorcerer is an example of a believing man who was not saved. The Scripture says: "Then Simon himself believed also: and . . . was baptized" (Acts 8:13). "But Peter said unto him . . . thy heart is not right in the sight of God. Repent therefore of this thy wickedness . . ." (Acts 8:20-22). Here is a man who believed all that demons believe, and was baptized, but without real repentance for sin. In fact, his faith did not take him as far as did that of the demons; for, says James, they "trembled": that is, they shuddered in terror at the coming judgment. Unquestionably, many in our churches stand and recite a creed week after week, saying, "I believe," but have no fear of God and of the judgment to come, never having been born again.

Saving faith is more than mental assent to truth; it is such a belief in the heart (Rom. 10:9) that the whole soul, or inner man, rests completely on Christ alone for salvation. Such faith is vastly more than mere speculative exercise of the mind. Salvation is free, but we can possess it only by a direct act of will and committal of ourselves to Christ by faith. Any faith that falls short of this is dead.

I recall having heard an evangelist illustrate saving faith. He imagined a tightrope walker pushing a wheelbarrow across a rope stretched between the Canadian and American sides of the Niagara Gorge. After walking across on the rope, he returned from the opposite side pushing a wheelbarrow. He turned to the crowd and asked: "Do you believe I can do it again?" The response from the crowd was almost spontaneous and affirmative. Then turning to a lad, he asked, "Do you believe that I can push the wheelbarrow across with you in it?" The young man replied, "Yes, I believe you can." "All right, climb in," said the acrobat. The young man was unwilling to do this and quickly stepped back to stand on the outside of the crowd. He believed the acrobat, but he was not willing to rest completely in the man. Personally, I would not blame the lad. There is One who said: ". . . Him that cometh to Me I will in no wise cast out" (John 6:37). "And I give unto them eternal life; and they shall never perish, neither shall any man pluck them out of my hand" (John 10:28). The Saviour has never failed to sustain any who cast their burden of sin upon Him. Commit yourself to Christ; trust completely in Him; cast yourself on Him, and He will see you safe to His Father's house.

Guy H. King, in a brief study on prepositions, points out the frequency with which the preposition "on" follows the verb "believe" when saving faith is being discussed. An example is found in Acts 16:31 ". . . Believe *on* the Lord Jesus Christ, and thou shalt be saved . . ." The same preposition is used in John 3:15, 16 where we find "in," and since it governs the accusative case it implies *motion toward,* or *on to,* the object. The true belief on Jesus Christ, then, is the quality of faith that takes you on to Him, to commit yourself to Him, to rest completely upon Him, to trust Him fully. This makes belief on Jesus Christ an acting faith, and it is essential to salvation. It is this "work" that makes the difference between a faith that is unto salvation and a faith that is not unto salvation. Personally, I feel that possibly James, by the Holy Spirit, takes up this point and penetrates more deeply into it than does Paul, though most assuredly Paul is not silent on it, for he testifies of the Thessalonian Christians that they "turned to God from idols" (1 Thess. 1:9). Theirs was a working faith—a faith that acted; they turned and went "on to" God.

Possibly there are some who would shout "heresy" at James's teaching as did Luther. But stop and think! Does James teach anything to contradict Paul? We have seen already that they agree, and must do so, for Paul too speaks of "your work of faith" (1 Thess. 1:3). Certainly Paul rejected the idea that salvation was by the works of the law or the works of the flesh; but he believed, like James, that only a working faith can save; and both Paul and James teach exactly what our Lord taught when He was here upon earth.

Christ reconciles Paul and James when He says: "This is the work of God, that ye believe on Him whom He hath sent" (John 6:29). This He said in answer to the question, "What shall we do, that we might work the works of God" (John 6:28)? A sin of the unregenerate, legalistic heart is to do its own works and then try to offer those works to God. The question they asked is the language of men occupied with themselves and their own doings. They wanted to do "works," thereby putting God in the position of debtor to them. But, as Paul writes, salvation is "not of *works*" (Eph. 2:9; Titus 3:5), but rather "*the work* of faith." and "this is *the work* . . . that ye believe on Him." The only one "work" that God will accept is faith in His Son. Nothing of man's doing can be added to the work of God in redemption. Only believe! This is your work of faith.

A dead faith that does not move you to place all your trust in Christ is no better than the faith of demons and will send you ultimately to hell with the demons. Look at verse 18. "Yea, a man may say, Thou hast faith, and I have works: shew me thy faith without thy works, and I will shew thee my faith by my works." Now both of these men claim to have faith. The one who says he has faith cannot substantiate his claim because his life shows no evidence of the work of faith. The other likewise claims to have faith, and while no man could read his heart, his "works" showed that his faith was a working faith. He had been saved by grace through faith and was now God's workmanship, created in Christ Jesus unto good works, which God hath before ordained that we should walk in them (Eph. 2:8-10). He knew that he was not saved by "works" (Titus 3:5), but he knew also that "they which have believed in God might be careful to maintain good works" (Titus 3:8). The work of faith in a true believer will be indicated and proved by good works according to the Scripture.

Are you truly God's child? Have you come to Christ and acknowledged that you are a pauper, a poor beggar unable to offer Him anything but a believing heart that will trust Him simply? If not, come at once without delay.

Is thy cruse of comfort failing?
  Rise and share it with a friend!
And through all the years of famine
  It shall serve thee to the end.
Love divine will fill thy storehouse,
  Or thy handful still renew;
Scanty fare for one will often
  Make a royal feast for two.

For the heart grows rich in giving:
  All its wealth is living grain;
Seeds—which mildew in the garner—
  Scattered, fill with gold the plain.
Is thy burden hard and heavy?
  Do thy steps drag wearily?
Help to lift thy brother's burden—
  God will bear both it and thee.

Is thy heart a well left empty?
  None but God its void can fill;
Nothing but a ceaseless fountain
  Can its ceaseless longings still.
Is thy heart a living power?
  Self-entwined, its strength sinks low;
It can only live by loving,
  And by serving love will grow.

CLARIFICATION THROUGH ILLUSTRATION

James 2:21-26

21. Was not Abraham our father justified by works, when he had offered Isaac his son upon the altar?

22. Seest thou how faith wrought with his works, and by works was faith made perfect?

23. And the scripture was fulfilled which saith, Abraham believed God, and it was imputed unto him for righteousness: and he was called the Friend of God.

24. Ye see then how that by works a man is justified, and not by faith only.

25. Likewise also was not Rahab the harlot justified by works, when she had received the messengers, and had sent them out another way?

26. For as the body without the spirit is dead, so faith without works is dead also.

In order to clarify his argument that a faith of words without works cannot save, James uses two practical illustrations of saving faith as found in the Old Testament and expounded in the New, namely, Abraham and Rahab. Having dealt with the work of faith, which is believing, James now turns to the works that proceed from genuine faith and which declare a man to be what he professes. The works in the verses before us are those that follow faith, having been produced by it.

Having in mind the Jews primarily, the Apostle could not have chosen a more illustrative character than Abraham. He is called in Scripture the father of the faithful, and the Jews were quite proud to refer to Abraham as their father. Because they were Jews after the flesh and believed in the God of Abraham, they felt a measure of security. Apparently they boasted often, saying: "We are Abraham's seed," and "Abraham is our father" (John 8:33, 39); but our Lord replied: "If ye were Abraham's

children, ye would do the works of Abraham" (John 8:39).
Those Jews, like many professing Christians today, made the
costly mistake of assuming that they automatically have a standing before God comparable to that of their believing parents.
Now James is going to show that Abraham not only believed
God, but that he did those things God told him to do, thereby
proving his faith by his works.

"Was not Abraham our father justified by works, when he
had offered Isaac his son upon the altar?" (James 2:21). Inter-
estingly enough Paul also was led by the Holy Spirit to use Abraham as an illustration. "What shall we say then that Abraham
our father, as pertaining to the flesh, hath found? For if Abraham were justified by works, he hath whereof to glory; but not
before God. For what saith the scripture? Abraham believed
God, and it was counted unto him for righteousness" (Rom.
4:1-3). "Even as Abraham believed God, and it was accounted
to him for righteousness. Know ye therefore that they which are
of faith, the same are the children of Abraham" (Gal. 3:6, 7).
Right here in these verses we have that seeming contradiction
between Paul and James. Actually the statements are not contradictory but complementary. A man is justified only by the
kind of faith which does the things that God commands. That
faith which refuses to obey God is not the faith that saves. Real
faith that saves is a faith that works.

I have been impressed with one of Paul's statements: namely,
"For if Abraham were justified by works, he hath whereof to
glory; *but not before God*" (Rom. 4:2). Do not fail to note those
words, *not before God*. There is one's justification before God
and one's justification before the world of men.

Now notice that James, in stating that Abraham was justified
by works, refers to the offering of Isaac by Abraham as recorded
in Genesis 22. James is not saying that Abraham was justified by
works, but rather that Abraham was justified by works *"when* he
had offered Isaac his son upon the altar." Do not overlook this
important time element since it is essential to a correct under-

standing of the context. Now take your Bible please and turn with me to Genesis 15:6. "And he [Abraham] believed in the Lord; and He counted it to him for righteousness." Note carefully that Abraham was justified by faith in God's eyes some forty years *before* he offered Isaac on Mount Moriah. We may see here that Abraham's justification by works in offering Isaac was not "before God." He was already declared righteous by God when he believed on the Lord. Paul, in Romans 4:2, is not saying that Abraham was justified by works, but he is saying that "*If* Abraham were justified by works," it is "not before God." As far as Abraham's standing before God was concerned, it was a matter of the heart only, for God alone knew whether or not his faith was real. James, on the other hand, is reminding us that Abraham's sacrificial works as recorded in Genesis 22, when he had offered up Isaac, justified him before men.

Neither Abraham, nor any other man, can attain the favor of God through any works of the flesh. No amount of works, no claims to perfect obedience will justify a sinner before God. Like Abraham, all men must *believe, trust, commit* themselves solely to God, and then God in grace will credit righteousness to their account on the ground of Christ's redemptive work at Calvary. Since God takes away from Abraham any right to claim justification on the ground of his own works, who among us can stand? Men today need to learn that God cannot accept self-righteousness. He will have none of it. The only righteousness acceptable unto God is that imputed righteousness which God Himself bestows upon the believing sinner, and that upon the faith principle only. My friends, if you and I are going to have any righteousness put to our account, God will have to put it there, for only on the ground of the finished work of our Lord Jesus Christ can God remain just, and the Justifier of those who believe in Jesus (Rom. 3:26). More important than having Abraham as our father in the *flesh* is to have him as our father in the *faith*. It is the all-glorious God-given privilege of all who come within range of the gospel message to receive the spiritual heritage of

Abraham. Believe on the Lord Jesus Christ, and thou shalt be saved.

There are works of the flesh, apart from salvation, that precede salvation; then there are the works of God, the fruit of the Spirit, which follow salvation, being produced by it. Paul looks at the *cause* of justification, and sees it from God's viewpoint. James looks at the *effects* of justification, and sees it from man's viewpoint. When Abraham was circumcised fourteen years after God justified him, Abraham proved by his actions that he truly believed God. When he led Isaac to the altar forty years after God had justified him, he proved once again his faith by his works. However, the works proved nothing to God, but proved his faith to man. God knew, apart from works, Abraham's faith was real; man, by Abraham's works, knew his faith was real.

"Seest thou how faith wrought with his works, and by works was faith made perfect?" (James 2:22). The Apostle appeals to reason. "Can't you see from this illustration of Abraham that faith and actions go hand in hand—that real faith is always supplemented by good works?" And this is what the Scripture means when it says: "Abraham believed God, and it was imputed unto him for righteousness: and he was called the Friend of God" (2:23). When the Bible says that Abraham believed God, you can count on that being genuine faith that produced good works; otherwise, God never would have written it of him. It is not what we say but what we do that proves the quality of our faith. When faith is genuine, it will obey God no matter how great the cost. In obedience to the divine command Abraham started by faith (Heb. 11:8), sojourned by faith (Heb. 11:9), and sacrificed by faith (Heb. 11:17). The Christian life, from its commencement, through its continuance, and unto its consummation is one of faith, the faith always being manifested by the fruits of obedience and good works.

Oh, my friends, what kind of faith do others see in us? James is appealing to professing believers to show forth the fruit of righteousness, which is the fruit of the Spirit. Whenever we see

Abraham's *faith* expressed in Scripture, we find it at *work;* and upon examining his works, we find they are produced by faith. Is our faith operative? Does it produce the fruit of works? Only by a faith that shows itself in good works can one be justified, whether before God or man. Our Lord said: "Wherefore by their fruits ye shall know them" (Matt. 7:16, 20). If every good tree bringeth forth good fruit, what of our lives? Whatever profession we may make, it is our lives that count. A man can be identified as to the genuineness of his faith only on the basis of what he produces. I may have a prophetical, a historical, a doctrinal knowledge of God's Divine Truth, but the real test of my profession is in my actions.

The other illustration from the Old Testament which James uses is that of Rahab. "Likewise also was not Rahab the harlot justified by works, when she had received the messengers, and had sent them out another way? For as the body without the spirit is dead, so faith without works is dead also" (2:25, 26). There is one other significant New Testament summary of the life of Rahab: "By faith the harlot Rahab perished not with them that believed not, when she had received the spies with peace" (Heb. 11:31). Both verses identify her as a harlot, and I take it that she was just that. This notorious Gentile woman, unable to claim birthright to those blessings that belonged to the seed of Abraham, has an interesting history. You may read about her in Joshua, Chapters 2 and 6. I am not treating lightly her awful sin, but I do rejoice to see how the worst of sinners can be forgiven and justified before God and man.

James is careful, as in his illustration with Abraham, to give the time when Rahab was justified by her works: "when she had received the messengers, and had sent them out another way." Rahab's own testimony, at the time of her good works, follows: "And she said unto the men, I know that the Lord hath given you the land, and that your terror is fallen upon us, and that all the inhabitants of the land faint because of you. For we have heard how the Lord dried up the water of the Red Sea for you, when ye came out of Egypt; and what ye did unto the two kings of the Amorites, that were on the other side Jordan, Sihon and Og, whom ye utterly destroyed" (Joshua 2:9, 10). When did she believe in the God of Israel? She had trusted her soul to Jehovah when she heard of His divine power in judgment against heathen nations. When she exercised that initial step of faith, she was justified before God. How long she trusted in God we are not told, but the day arrived when she proved her faith by her works and not merely by her words. When she hid the spies she was justified by her works before men.

Robert Johnstone in his lectures points out that the position James is maintaining is that all justifying faith is operative. The very nature of saving faith demands that good works follow regardless of the nature of the case before one is saved. The two illustrations by James show the consistent effectiveness of the gospel at all times. Here both sexes are reached. Here two extremes of moral behavior are seen. Here the grace of God is doing its work in the hearts of Jew and Gentile alike. No matter what one's past has been, religiously, morally, socially, or otherwise, if any one will truly and sincerely believe on the Lord Jesus Christ, he shall be saved. If he is truly saved, good works, according to the Word of God, will follow.

Now a word in conclusion. "For as the body without the spirit is dead, so faith without works is dead also" (2:26). When a person dies, the body becomes lifeless because the spirit, or breath, has left it. A dead body is good for nothing. Unless it is soon buried it will spread stench and disease. Even so a mere profession of faith in Jesus Christ that does not produce good works is dead also. We know there is life in a body when breathing action can be detected. We know that faith is alive when we see it acting. Abraham and Rahab proved their faith by their works. What does your profession of faith prove? Do you claim to be a true believer in Jesus Christ? If so, "be careful to maintain good works" (Titus 3:8).

Being a minister of God's Word, I must remind you with Paul

that works, without a dynamic, living faith in the Lord Jesus Christ, cannot produce salvation. On the other hand, I must remind you with James that a formal faith in declaring a dogma or confessing a creed that fails to produce life and labor according to the Word of God, will likewise condemn you.

The writer of these pages takes this opportunity to thank God once again for the second chapter of James.

Fading away like the stars of the morning,
  Losing their light in the glorious sun—
Thus would we pass from the earth and its toiling,
  Only remembered by what we have done.

Shall we be missed, though by others succeeded,
  Reaping the fields we in springtime have sown?
Yes, but the sowers must pass from their labors,
  Ever remembered by what they have done.

Only the truth that in life we have spoken,
  Only the seed that on earth we have sown;
These shall pass onward when we are forgotten,
  Fruits of the harvest and what we have done.

Oh, when the Saviour shall make up His jewels,
  When the bright crowns of rejoicing are won,
Then shall His weary and faithful disciples
  All be remembered by what they have done.

Only remembered, only remembered,
  Only remembered by what we have done;
Thus would we pass from the earth and its toiling,
  Only remembered by what we have done.

RETRIBUTION THROUGH
RESPONSIBILITY

James 3:1-2

1. My brethren, be not many masters, knowing that we shall receive the greater condemnation.

2. For in many things we offend all. If any man offend not in word, the same is a perfect man, and able also to bridle the whole body.

There is every indication that James had a reason for going into this present discourse on the right and wrong use of the tongue. In the first two chapters, especially Chapter Two, the Apostle placed emphasis upon *works* and not *words*. He spoke plainly of those who *say* they have faith but do not show the fruits of faith. Now lest there be those who might be led to feel that it makes no difference what we say, James proceeds to show that words *are* important.

This author is thoroughly convinced that no portion of the Epistle of James is more urgently needed in our churches than this section before us. There are many earnest Christians who consider themselves to be utterly unaware of the ways in which they sin with the tongue. These same Christians cringe from the very thoughts of using tobacco, dancing, card playing, attending the theater, and the like, but they engage in talebearing, gossip, slander, and backbiting. I consider the teaching in James, Chapter Three, to be a key to the solution of most of the ills in church life today.

James mentions the tongue in every chapter (1:19, 26; 2:12; 4:11, 5:12), but in Chapter Three he expands and expounds more fully his subject. Here the Holy Spirit sums up and brings together the Scriptural teaching on the sacredness of speech, for by the "tongue" James most certainly has in mind the gift of speech. In our reading and study of the Scriptures we come across certain chapters which seem to contain the sum total of Biblical teaching on a given subject. James Three is one such chapter.

"My brethren, be not many masters, knowing that we shall receive the greater condemnation" (James 3:1). Thus far in his Epistle the Apostle has used the words "My brethren" three times. These appear at the beginning of each of the first three chapters (1:2; 2:1; 3:1). In addition he addresses his readers three times as "My beloved brethren" (1:16, 19; 2:5). I do not believe that he is guilty of hypocrisy: that is, of using a "nice' phrase in order to cover up a tirade against them. His hear was in his message, his one desire being to offer spiritual help t his brethren in Christ.

"Be not many masters." It is to be feared that our modern u;e of the English word "master" has led some to attach a wrong meaning to it here. The generally accepted use of the word conveys the idea of superiority and rule over another. But such is not always the case. The idea most prominent in our text is that of "instructor" or "teacher." We see this in our Lord's words to Nicodemus, "Art thou a *master* of Israel, and knowest not these things?" (John 3:10). His injunction is that not every one in the assembly should seek to teach instead of learn. In Chapter Two (verses 19-25) he exhorted them to learn and live the Word of God.

The synagogues in those days were places of open discussions where everyone who desired might come forward to speak his mind. Paul himself, even after his conversion, had free access to these forum places on the Sabbath day where he witnessed to the Person, Word, and Work of Jesus Christ. The Apostle to the Gentiles wrote later: "How is it then, brethren? when ye come together, every one of you hath a psalm, hath a doctrine, hath a tongue, hath a revelation, hath an interpretation. Let all things be done unto edifying" (1 Cor. 14:26).

Human nature has not changed since the time of Paul and James. It seems quite natural even in our time for many to want to lecture others rather than to be learners. If the local assembly had no teacher, the situation would be bad indeed, but perhaps it is far worse when everyone wants to teach and no one desires to be taught. Our proper place in the assembly should be manifestly that of ready listeners and learners. I see the great need among brethren to cultivate a teachable spirit. The pride of Scriptural knowledge has made men arrogant and critical. Some Christians seldom receive a blessing in the public worship and teaching service because they did not come to be taught, but rather to judge the content and composition of the speaker's message.

The office of teacher is a divinely appointed one. The ascended Lord, in bestowing gifts to the Church, gave some to be pastors and teachers (Eph. 4:11), but when a large group in any assembly give themselves to lecturing rather than learning, and their time to the regulation of the affairs of others rather than to the regulation of their own affairs, much harm is certain to result.

But why do we seek to be teachers rather than to be taught? Is it for the influence and authority that seemingly go with the teaching position? To covet the authority of a teacher is a Pharisaical sin. Our Lord rebuked the Pharisees for such when He said: "But all their works they do for to be seen of men: they make broad their phylacteries, and enlarge the borders of their garments, And love the uppermost rooms at feasts, and the chief seats in the synagogues, And greetings in the markets, and to be called of men, Rabbi [teacher], Rabbi [teacher]. But be not ye called Rabbi [teacher]: for one is your Master, even Christ; and all ye are brethren" (Matt. 23:5-8). We need to be delivered from the flair of self-appointed critics who are merely novices.

When James warns his readers against becoming too eager to teach others, he does so on the ground that as such their responsibility is greater in this life, and that any failure on their part will result in greater loss at the Judgment Seat of Christ: *"Knowing that we shall receive the greater condemnation* [judgment]."

The abuse of any privilege involves guilt; likewise the abuse of greater and larger responsibility involves greater guilt. God is going to require from each of us in proportion to the responsibility to which we are called in the Body of Christ, "For unto whomsoever much is given, of him shall be much required; and to whom men have committed much, of him they will ask the more" (Luke 12:48). The recognized instructor of others who attempts to influence men for good, needs to spend much time in prayer and with the Word of God. Far greater judgment awaits him who is not a faithful teacher than that to which his listeners are exposed.

A teacher of others, among whom this writer includes himself, might well reflect soberly upon this teaching every time he attempts to instruct others. Calvin writes: "He imposes a hard law on himself, who tries the words and deeds of others according to the rule of extreme rigour." Let every teacher of children and adults take heed. When we teach the Word of God we handle sublime and eternal truth. Let every lesson, every message, spoken or written, be given much time in thought and prayer. Ponder the solemn words of the Lord to His servant Ezekiel: "Son of man, I have made thee a watchman unto the house of Israel: therefore hear the word at my mouth, and give them warning from me. When I say unto the wicked, Thou shalt surely die; and thou givest him not warning, nor speakest to warn the wicked from his wicked way, to save his life; the same wicked man shall die in his iniquity; but his blood will I require at thine hand" (Ezek. 3:17, 18). Let these words apply to us in all of their divine import, for the measure of our failure determines the measure of the judgment that awaits us. Can we say with the Apostle Paul: "Wherefore I take you to record this day, that I am pure from the blood of all men. For I have not shunned to declare unto you all the counsel of God" (Acts 20:26, 27)?

Before we seek to set others right, let us make sure our own hearts are right.

In summing up verse one I suggest three lessons to be learned. First, unless God has endowed us with the gift of teaching, let us not presume to take a place in the assembly to which we are not called, but let us seek to occupy humbly and quietly the place for which God has fitted us. Second, we have no right to exercise ourselves in teaching others if the truth taught is not practiced by us. "Therefore thou art inexcusable, O man, whosoever thou art that judgest: for wherein thou judgest another, thou condemnest thyself; for thou that judgest doest the same things" (Rom. 2:1). Third, if God has called us to serve in the capacity of speaking to others, we have a solemn responsibility never to shirk our calling.

We come now to a sound reason why we should move slowly to teach and advise others: "For in many things we offend all . . ." (3:2). The idea here is not that we offend every one to whom we minister, but that we all offend. Actually James is saying, "in many things we all offend." None of God's children is perfect. We all are guilty of stumbling in many things. There are no perfect people who always remain guiltless of a slip of the tongue, or who never utter an idle or angry word. In the matter of the believer's words and works James sets the standard high, but he is no perfectionist. Now there are some very sensitive people who will be offended at even the things we do and say that are right, but the Apostle does not have such hypercritical persons in mind. I believe he is alluding to the fact that the choicest saints are not always right in what they do and say.

Job was a very good man with God's recommendation to back him up (Job 1:8), but Job confessed how easy it was for him to sin with the tongue. Hear him! "Behold, I am vile; what shall I answer thee? I will lay mine hand upon my mouth" (Job 40:4).

Isaiah was a good and godly servant of Jehovah; still he confessed: "I am undone; because I am a man of unclean lips . . .

Then flew one of the seraphims unto me, having a live coal in his hand, which he had taken with the tongs from off the altar: And he laid it upon my mouth, and said, Lo, this hath touched thy lips; and thine iniquity is taken away, and thy sin purged" (Isaiah 6:5-7).

Peter was a disciple of Jesus Christ. One day he boasted: ". . . Though all men shall be offended because of thee, yet will I never be offended" (Matt. 26:33). But that very night Peter sinned with his tongue when he denied his Lord and cursed (Matt. 26:69-75).

Moses was certainly one of God's truly great men, but it is written of him "that he spake unadvisedly with his lips" (Psalm 106:33).

Paul, the great Apostle to the Gentiles, confessed: "For I know that in me (that is, in my flesh,) dwelleth no good thing . . ." (Rom. 7:18). See him fail with his tongue in an outburst of self-defense as he shouted to Ananias the high priest: "God shall smite thee, thou whited wall" (Acts 23:1-5). His apology showed him to be in the wrong, but the damage had been done and his words could not be recalled.

I am afraid that none of us can stand in matters pertaining to the right and wrong use of the tongue. In this we all have sinned and do sin. None but our blessed Lord remained faultless, for He "did no sin, neither was guile found in his mouth: Who, when he was reviled, reviled not again" (1 Peter 2:22, 23).

The control of the tongue is the barometer of Christian maturity. The speech of any Christian will soon reveal whether or not he is spiritual, for "If any man offend not in word, the same is a perfect man, and able also to bridle the whole body." James is telling us that if a person could be found who was never guilty of uttering a faulty expression, he would be a well-balanced and thoroughly mature man, able to control the rest of his body.

The word "perfect" contains the idea of *full grown*. The perfect man referred to in Scripture is not one who has his old nature eradicated, but rather one who has grown to spiritual and moral maturity. Such growth to maturity can come only as one drinks deeply of the Word of God (1 Peter 2:2). "Brethren, be not children in understanding: howbeit in malice be ye children, but in understanding be men" (1 Cor. 14:20). Control of one's speech does not in itself constitute perfection, or spiritual maturity, but it is certainly one test as to whether a Christian is or is not growing.

Are we like little children, young men, or adults (1 John 2:12-14)? Since maturity is judged by our speech, how many of us claim full stature? As I ponder seriously these verses in James, I must confess that the tongue is most difficult for me to control. I have found it possible to control other parts of my body more readily than I have been able to conquer the expression of words. If an unbridled tongue gives evidence of an unbridled heart, and our Lord said that it does (Matt. 12:34), there is need for much heart searching among brethren in Christ. It is a false sanctity that takes pride in refraining from those things that are seemingly more odious but which bites and devours others with words.

Speech is one of the highest distinctions, between man and lower forms of animals. Only man can express his thoughts in articulate language and in writing. Science has produced many remarkable types of recording machines whereby the very tones of the human voice, even to a whisper, can be preserved for many years to come. The idea originated with God. The Bible says: "But I say unto you, That every idle word that men shall speak, they shall give account thereof in the day of judgment. For by thy words thou shalt be justified, and by thy words thou shalt be condemned" (Matt. 12:36, 37). Oh, beloved brethren, let us learn the first lesson in Christian living as expressed by David: "I said, I will take heed to my ways, that I sin not with my tongue: I will keep my mouth with a bridle, while the wicked is before me" (Psalm 39:1).

I once read of a native who, after confessing Christ, came to the missionary at the station compound offering himself for

Christian service. The missionary told his young Christian friend that he should learn by heart Psalm 39:1, then return when he felt he had learned that lesson and had put it into practice. At the end of one month the native returned to report many failures but some small progress. For almost a year the native returned month after month always reporting some progress but finally able to see that the bridling of the tongue involves a lifetime of discipline.

Socrates said to a young student: "Speak, friend, that I may see thee." Remember, Christian brothers and sisters, our speech reveals our hearts.

Only a little word, softly and kindly
  Breathed in the ear of the sad and opprest;
Oh, how it tenderly steals like a melody
  Over life's billows, and lulls them to rest!

Only a little word, softly and kindly
  Dropped in a heart that is blighted and chilled;
Oh, how its gentle strain tunes every chord again;
  Waking the echoes that sorrow has stilled!

Only a little word! Only a little word!
Only a little word, whispered in love!

TESTED THROUGH
THE TONGUE

James 3:3-12

3. Behold, we put bits in the horses' mouths, that they may obey us; and we turn about their whole body.

4. Behold also the ships, which though they be so great, and are driven of fierce winds, yet are they turned about with a very small helm, whithersoever the governor listeth.

5. Even so the tongue is a little member, and boasteth great things. Behold, how great a matter a little fire kindleth!

6. And the tongue is a fire, a world of iniquity: so is the tongue among our members, that it defileth the whole body, and setteth on fire the course of nature; and it is set on fire of hell.

7. For every kind of beasts, and of birds, and of serpents, and of things in the sea, is tamed, and hath been tamed of mankind:

8. But the tongue can no man tame; it is an unruly evil, full of deadly poison.

9. Therewith bless we God, even the Father; and therewith curse we men, which are made after the similitude of God.

10. Out of the same mouth proceedeth blessing and cursing. My brethren, these things ought not so to be.

11. Doth a fountain send forth at the same place sweet water and bitter?

12. Can the fig tree, my brethren, bear olive berries? either a vine, figs? so can no fountain both yield salt water and fresh.

Our Epistle abounds in illustrations. If the writers of the Scriptures revealed their individual native gifts and personalities, and we believe that they did, then James was possessed of an observing and analogical mind. He used commonplace things to illustrate divine truth. In this he was very much like our Lord, for Jesus Himself taught by analogy, using the little child, the sower, the wheat and tares, the wedding garment, the lighted candle, the wineskins, the children playing in the market place,

and many others. The Epistle of James shows that he borrowed
much both from the teachings and teaching methods of our Lord
Jesus Christ. Thus far we have seen his effective use of the wave
of the sea, the wind, the sun, the grass, and the mirror. Now he
speaks of the horse and its bridle, the ship and its helm, the fire
and its fuel, the beasts, birds, serpents, and fish.

Keep in mind that the main subject before us is the dangerous
misuse of the tongue. This message, though written nineteen
hundred years ago, might have been addressed to our own generation. These sins of the tongue are no less common among believers today than when James wrote about them. Perhaps there
never has been, at any time, a part of man so difficult to control
as the tongue.

We are to see now how the tongue controls and guides the
whole course of life. "Behold, we put bits in the horses' mouths,
that they may obey us; and we turn about their whole body"
(3:3). Has it ever occurred to you just how remarkably effective
a small bit and bridle are when placed in the mouth of a horse?
With their use one man can hold in check a team of several
horses, without which a hundred men could not control them.
The lesson to be learned here is that man can direct a strong
creature merely by controlling its tongue. If a horse is not broken
to bit and bridle as a young colt, it will run wild with its mis-
directed strength. Command the mouth of the horse and you
command the whole horse.

Now how does this illustration apply to us? The tongue,
though small and seemingly insignificant, if left to go unbridled,
results in an uncontrolled man. That man's life will be unchecked
and unguided. A horse controlled by a bit can render a great
service, but uncontrolled it can render much harm. A tongue,
controlled by the Lord Jesus Christ, can be a great blessing, but
an uncontrolled tongue will do much damage.

When I was a student in seminary a certain professor, who
was an anti-dispensationalist, told his class one day that if any
student owned a Scofield Reference Bible, his advice to that

student would be to burn it. There was in that classroom a young man who said he felt led to prepare for the Christian ministry. Before he left home, upon graduating from high school, his mother, a devout Christian, gave her boy a Scofield Bible. That student followed the advice of an unbridled tongue and burned his Scofield Bible. One year later he left the seminary, his mind full of doubt and uncertainty, and is to this day, as far as I have knowledge, a defeated and disillusioned man. If that professor would have had a bridled tongue he might have been used to guide a young life. He hurt not only others but himself as well. Yes, the tongue of one person can exercise dominion over many lives. If the tongue is given control it will imperil someone's future for time and eternity.

The next illustration is that of a ship's rudder. "Behold also the ships, which though they be so great, and are driven of fierce winds, yet are they turned about with a very small helm whithersoever the governor listeth" (3:4). A great vessel laden with passengers and cargo is brought safely to port because the vessel is made to go wherever the steersman may wish. A rudder, though very small, can control the destiny of all aboard that vessel. This illustration, like the former, seeks to show that the tongue, though small, is powerful enough to control the destiny of man. Many an unfortunate soul is out on life's sea, driven with the wind and tossed. He needs a word of counsel, of cheer, of comfort. Such a word could be used to guide the troubled soul to safe harbor. You see how the tongue, properly controlled, has a great ministry in guiding others. Did you ever pause to think that the little tongue in your mouth plays a role comparable in importance to the steering apparatus on the largest ocean vessel? Well, it does! James makes no extravagant statement, then, when he states that the one who governs his tongue will thereby regulate his whole life.

In verse five the two illustrations are applied. "Even so the tongue is a little member, and boasteth great things. Behold, how great a matter a little fire kindleth!" The tongue may be a little member, but do not underestimate the possible extent of its destructive powers. Look at how large a forest fire might result from one little spark. The word "matter" is better translated to mean "wood" or "forest." A single little spark from a locomotive, a match, a lighted cigarette, or a campfire has been known to destroy many acres of valuable timber. Yes, and quite often a little word, angrily or carelessly spoken, has caused war engulfing nations in bloodshedding, division of a once strong testimony for Christ, and sent husbands and wives to the divorce courts. Do we realize that the tongue is the most active member of the entire body used to communicate with others? This makes it capable of performing the greatest variety of good or the greatest variety of evil.

It is doubtful as to whether there is anything in nature more destructive than fire. The liquid fire from one single volcanic eruption has been known to bury completely an entire city. The great Chicago fire in 1871 destroyed almost one-half of the city and made almost 125,000 persons homeless. In 1953 a pan of rice boiled over onto a charcoal stove in a small home in Korea. Before twenty-four hours had passed almost 3,000 buildings were completely destroyed within an area covering one square mile. "Behold, how great a matter a little fire kindleth!"

"And the tongue is a fire, a world of iniquity: so is the tongue among our members, that it defileth the whole body, and setteth on fire the course of nature; and it is set on fire of hell" (3:6). Words spoken carelessly, unwisely, destructively, can set ablaze the whole sphere of our existence, affecting seriously our family life, church life, and community life. This destructive power of the tongue is satanic: "It is set on fire of hell." Can language be clearer and stronger than this? I beg of you to share with me the seriousness and solemnness of these words of James. Behind every word that is unclean, untrue, angry, divisive, unkind, is Satan himself. I know of one family that has been divided and whose members have not spoken to one another for almost twenty years, all the result of a few unkind words. In this particular instance the tongue has defiled every member of the family. Indeed "it defileth the whole body." The untempered heat of the tongue has marred many a vessel, rendering it unfit for the Master's use.

Mountain climbers have said that there are certain times and places when the vibration from a faint whisper could bring down an avalanche. Whenever the guide detects such sensitivity in the air, he cautions every climber to remain silent. Our Lord said: "Not that which goeth into the mouth defileth a man; but that which cometh out of the mouth, this defileth a man" (Matt. 15:11). Oh, let us not be guilty of sinning with the tongue. The wickedness of the tongue emanates from the abyss and it is ignited by Satan with the very fires of hell. An avalanche of sorrow and separation may be caused from the faintest whisper of gossip, slander, lying, jealousy, bitterness, and the like. "An ungodly man diggeth up evil: and in his lips there is as a burning fire" (Prov. 16:27).

There comes to my mind that remarkable incident which occurred on the day of Pentecost. As the disciples waited prayerfully, their tongues were set on fire of the Holy Spirit and they began to speak as the Spirit gave them utterance. The multitudes marvelled as they heard them speak "the wonderful works of God" (Acts 2:3-11). Let our tongues be controlled by the Holy Spirit and we too will be speaking forth the praises of the Lord.

The Apostle continues his use of illustrations by referring to animal life. "For every kind of beasts, and of birds, and of serpents, and of things in the sea, is tamed, and hath been tamed of mankind" (3:7). Here he reminds us how the worst and deadliest of wild beasts have been tamed by men. The writer has seen demonstrations of man's skill in taming huge porpoises of the sea, wild birds of the jungle, and ferocious beasts of the forests. Only recently he witnessed a demonstration of a tamed cobra. When God created our first parents He gave them dominion over the animals (Gen. 1:28; Psalm 8:6-8). It is quite possible that this dominion was exercised more fully before the fall of man, but since the fall he has continued to prove his ability.

Now notice the contrast between wild animals and man's tongue. "But the tongue can no man tame; it is an unruly evil, full of deadly poison" (3:8). Man can tame the fiercest beasts, but no man can tame the tongue. Do not read into this verse something that is not here. The verse does not say that the tongue cannot be tamed. It does declare emphatically, however, that no *man* can tame it. By nature the gift of speech is more difficult to control than are the fiercest of beasts. There were times when I felt confidently that I had my tongue well controlled, but then it cut loose with words which only proved conclusively the truth in the verse before us. We all have learned from experience that no powers of the natural man are adequate to control the tongue, promises and resolutions notwithstanding. Let me be frank in my application of this verse and say that in the matter of insubordination, man is worse than the beasts.

While no *man* can tame the tongue, there is One who can. The Lord is no less able to control a lying, blaspheming, slanderous, gossiping tongue than He is to deliver the drunkard from alcohol, the gambler from the game table, the narcotics addict from drugs, or the lustful person from adultery. Yet, I have witnessed in the lives of not a few converts that it was much easier to forsake these things than to get victory over a wicked tongue.

There is a reason why. Even after we are brought to know the Lord, the old corrupt nature inherited from our first parents is still with us. True, all believers have been the recipients of the divine nature received through the incoming of the Holy Spirit, but there is never an eradication of the old nature.

A Christian's two natures must not be confused with "human nature." Every man and every woman possess a human nature. Adam had a human nature before and after his fall. Our Lord Jesus Christ had a human nature.

Every human being born by natural processes inherits a fallen sinful nature from his parents and upon becoming a child of God, the believer becomes the battleground of a conflict between the old nature (self), and the new nature (the Holy Spirit). Our blessed Lord was the only exception. He was supernaturally conceived by the Holy Spirit with no human father. Only those who are born of the Spirit, new creatures in Christ Jesus, possess the new nature. These natures are contrary one toward the other, expressed in the Bible as follows: "For the flesh lusteth against the Spirit, and the Spirit against the flesh: and these are contrary the one to the other: so that ye cannot do the things that ye would" (Galatians 5:17). Many years after he was saved the Apostle Paul testified: "For I know that in me (that is, in my flesh,) dwelleth no good thing: for to will is present with me; but how to perform that which is good I find not" (Rom. 7:18). By the presence of the Holy Spirit dwelling in us, and by careful attention to the study of, and obedience to the Word of God provision has been made that we need not sin. When, however, some sin, some weakness, some former habit overtakes us, we must come at once to God in prayer and confess our wrong. He will forgive and cleanse us (1 John 1:9), and give grace to go on in practical holiness (Heb. 4:16).

We must exercise great care and be much in prayer in regard to our use of the tongue, for, says James: "It is an unruly evil, full of deadly poison." The word "unruly" suggests the idea of instability and restlessness. And how restless and unstable the tongue is! It is difficult to hold it still, and when it does speak we cannot depend upon its words being the right words. Like a serpent, it is armed with venom, a deadly and death-bringing poison. "Their throat is an open sepulchre; with their tongues they have used deceit; the poison of asps is under their lips: Whose mouth is full of cursing and bitterness" (Rom. 3:13, 14).

Guy H. King writes: "The deadly drug does not need to be taken in large doses—a drop or two will suffice; and the tongue does not need to distil long speeches, it has but to drop a word, and the mischief is set afoot. Thus has a peace been ruined, thus has a reputation been blackened, thus has a friendship been embittered, thus has a mind been poisoned, thus has a life been blasted. Let a child's rhyme point the same moral—

'I lost a very little word, only the other day;
It was a very naughty word I had not meant to say.
But, then, it was not really lost—when from my lips it flew,
My little brother picked it up, and now he says it too!' "

One wrong whispered word may spoil a reputation, smear a character, and even destroy the usefulness of a life. My Christian friends, let us begin each day with the prayer of the Psalmist: "Set a watch, O Lord, before my mouth; keep the door of my lips" (Psalm 141:3), lest this unrestrainable, ungovernable instrument of evil, highly charged with deadly poison work its destructive powers on us. Crossbones and skull are the accepted marks appearing on any container warning of poison in the contents. Before you speak remember the crossbones and skull.

The context shows us how unnaturally inconsistent the tongue really is. This lesson is illustrated by use of a fountain. "Therewith bless we God, even the Father; and therewith curse we men, which are made after the similitude of God. Out of the same mouth proceedeth blessing and cursing. My brethren, these things ought not so to be" (3:9, 10). As I meditated upon these verses they left me with a sick feeling as I saw the awful reality of my inconsistency when failing to control my tongue. Here two uses of the tongue are set in contrast to each other. On the one hand, we exercise the tongue in its noblest and loftiest use, namely, to praise God. Then on the other hand, we exercise the same member in its most degrading and injurious use, namely, to speak evil of man. How utterly sinful it is to bless our God and heavenly Father with the very tongue we use to call His anathema down upon any man whom He has created in His own image.

If you are loud in your praises of God, do not commit the heinous sin of speaking evil of men. Do you honestly feel you have been face to face with God in singing His praises, reading

His Word, and in prayer, if when you go home you show an irritated, undisciplined, angry temper by scolding, condemning, and finding fault with your tongue? Such a temper shuts us out from the presence of God. We preachers have been telling our audiences how sinful Peter was when he praised His Lord (Matt. 16:16) and cursed in denial of Him within so short a period of time (Matt. 26:74). But how many professing Christians are there who are no less sinful than was Peter?

To bless and praise the Lord is the highest possible use of our tongues. The Christian is exhorted throughout the Scriptures to praise God. This is set forth fully in the Psalms. But if you think you can praise the Lord on Sunday and engage in any form of evil speaking on weekdays, you are a liar according to God's Word (1 John 4:20), deceiving your own heart (James 1:26). Stop it! Oh, fellow Christian, let us stop it! We have no right to utter an unkind, ill-tempered word against any, even if that person has wronged us. Leave those who have injured you in God's hands. "Dearly beloved, avenge not yourselves, but rather give place unto wrath: for it is written, Vengeance is mine; I will repay, saith the Lord. Therefore if thine enemy hunger, feed him; if he thirst, give him drink: for in so doing thou shalt heap coals of fire on his head. Be not overcome of evil, but overcome evil with good" (Rom. 12:19-21).

On one occasion James and John, seeking to serve the Lord, said: "Lord, wilt thou that we command fire to come down from heaven, and consume them, even as Elias did? But he turned, and rebuked them, and said, Ye know not what manner of spirit ye are of" (Luke 9:54, 55). Now, writing against this very thing, the Holy Spirit says: "My brethren, these things ought not so to be." Indeed they *ought not*. Paul wrote: "And withal they learn to be idle, wandering about from house to house; and not only idle, but tattlers also and busybodies, speaking things which they *ought not*" (1 Tim. 5:13). The Apostle to the Gentiles has given us another "ought not" of the tongue: "For there are many unruly and vain talkers and deceivers, specially they of the circumcision: Whose mouths must be stopped, who subvert whole houses, teaching things which they *ought not,* for filthy lucre's sake" (Titus 1:10, 11). These verses make it clear that we *ought not* to gossip at any time nor under any circumstance. May God help us to determine in our hearts that, by His grace and power, we *shall not.*

"Doth a fountain send forth at the same place sweet water and bitter?" (3:11). No one ever yet drew both pure and brakish water from the same spigot. The very thought of such a thing is contrary to all nature. Just as no fountain can yield salt water and fresh at the same place, even so can no professing believer in Jesus Christ justify his profession if his tongue goes undisciplined. The laws of nature cry out against such falsity. Yet we can sit in a public meeting and send forth the sweet water of praise to God and go out to our homes and speak forth the bitter water of angry speech. What strange and paradoxical things we Christians do!

Possibly you are convicted even now by the Holy Spirit. Your bitter words trouble you. Let me remind you of an incident that occurred during the journey of the children of Israel from Egypt to Canaan. When they came to Marah, they could not drink the water because it was bitter. Then Moses turned to God in prayer, and the Lord showed him a *tree* which, when he had cast it into the waters, made the waters sweet (Exodus 15:23-25). That tree is a type of another Tree, the Cross upon which our blessed Lord suffered and died for sin (1 Peter 2:24). Yes, the Cross will sweeten the flow of our speech; it will heal the poison of a bitter tongue. Turn now to the Lord Jesus Christ for help, confess your sin, and the bitter shall be made sweet.

The final illustration in this section is likewise drawn from nature. "Can the fig tree, my brethren, bear olive berries? either a vine, figs? so can no fountain both yield salt water and fresh" (3:12). It is unnatural and even impossible for a fig tree to grow olives, or a grapevine to grow figs. Each must produce after its kind. You may draw the only possible conclusion. Since like begets like, evil speech can only emanate from an evil heart. The heart of man obeys laws as fixed as that law by which the fig tree bears figs and the vine bears grapes. Every tree is known by its fruit, and out of the abundance of the heart the mouth speaketh. Indeed the tongue is a test of life.

I am not skilled to understand
What God hath willed, what God hath planned;
I only know at His right hand
Is One who is my Saviour!

I take Him at His word indeed:
"Christ died for sinners"—this I read;
For in my heart I find a need
Of Him to be my Saviour!

That He should leave His place on high,
And come for sinful man to die,
You count it strange?—so once did I,
Before I knew my Saviour.

And Oh, that He fulfilled may see
The travail of His soul in me,
And with His work contented be,
As I with my dear Saviour!

Yes, living, dying, let me bring
My strength, my solace from this spring—
That He who lives to be my King
Once died to be my Saviour!

HOLY WORKS THROUGH
HEAVENLY WISDOM

James 3:13-18

13. Who is a wise man and endued with knowledge among you? let him shew out of a good conversation his works with meekness of wisdom.

14. But if ye have bitter envying and strife in your hearts, glory not, and lie not against the truth.

15. This wisdom descendeth not from above, but is earthly, sensual, devilish.

16. For where envying and strife is, there is confusion and every evil work.

17. But the wisdom that is from above is first pure, then peaceable, gentle, and easy to be intreated, full of mercy and good fruits, without partiality, and without hypocrisy.

18. And the fruit of righteousness is sown in peace of them that make peace.

The verses in this section of Chapter Three have a closer connection with the preceding than might be realized at first. These words contain an appeal to the reader to pursue true heavenly wisdom, which is from above in contrast to earthly wisdom, which is "devilish." Our chapter opened with an address to those who would be teachers, and who, because of that worthy office, were usually looked upon as wise men. Let us keep in our minds the fact that James is writing to Christians; therefore the first force of the application must be applied to the Christian heart.

A vast difference exists between the wisdom of man and the wisdom of God. Worldly-wise men are often proud of their self-gained knowledge, eager for discussion and disputation, and sometimes more eager to defeat others by their arguments. Wisdom, according to the world's standards, is a certain cleverness which enables one to defeat one's opponent by words, thereby gaining one's own way and winning a point. Such wisdom is not from above and has not God's approval. The wisdom which one asks and receives of God according to James 1:5 has certain marks of godliness upon it.

"Who is a wise man and endued with knowledge among you? let him shew out of a good conversation his works with meekness of wisdom" (3:13). The question is most challenging. It does not condemn all its readers as though they were not truly wise, but rather it does arrest the attention of those who had been loudest in self-esteem. Doubtless there were those in James's day (and ours) who, if honest, would come up with the answer. *"We* are." None of us wants to be put on record as being undiscerning and lacking in understanding. Yet, those of us who have thought ourselves to be men and women of wisdom must confess that too many times we failed to judge soundly and to deal sagaciously with facts.

In substance the Apostle's meaning is as follows: "If you are truly wise according to God's standard of wisdom, you will show your wisdom by a holy and meek life." We are not asked to *speak* convincingly but to *show* the works of wisdom. Genuine Christian wisdom, according to God's standard, finds expression in one's daily course of life and conduct. "Let him shew out of a good conversation his works with meekness of wisdom." The word "conversation," in modern English, means the exchange of thought through speech, but at the time the King James Version of the Bible was translated, it meant "manner of life or conduct." Conversation here means more than talk; it means walk. It means more than words; it means works. The believer's walk, or manner of life, if it is to be in wisdom, must be according to God's Word. Paul tells us that the Holy Scriptures are able to make us wise (2 Tim. 3:15). The "conversation," or behavior, of the wise Christian will be as (1) becometh the gospel (Phil. 1:27), (2) honest (1 Pet. 2:12), (3) chaste (1 Pet. 3:1, 2), (4) without covetousness (Heb. 13:5). To speak well is fine, but it is not enough. To be endued with the knowledge of God's Word is commendable, but such knowledge must be practical in our daily lives, else we are not wise. Knowledge is the possession of facts; wisdom is the proper use and application of knowledge.

Heavenly wisdom is marked by "meekness." A wisdom that is not meek is not the real thing; it is not from above. This marked note of difference will distinguish the counterfeit wisdom from the true. Different expositors have given several interpretations of this word "meekness." Personally, I like the idea of *modesty*. In 1:21 the hearer of the Word is exhorted to receive it with meekness, and now we are exhorted to manifest that same modesty of mind. Common courtesy and sweet reasonableness are missing virtues among many believers today. Arrogance and presumption prevail on every hand. We need the retiring and restraining influence of the Holy Spirit in our lives. Peter pleads for this same spirit even among those who are called to defend the faith (1 Pet. 3:15). The wise man does not puff himself up, nor does he parade his knowledge.

In the remaining verses of our chapter, James contrasts earthly wisdom with heavenly wisdom. First, he deals with earthly wisdom (verses 14-16). It is marked by "bitter envying and strife in your hearts." The words *"but if ye have"* imply that this condition actually existed. They claimed faith in God's Word, but they were *harshly jealous* and *selfishly ambitious*. Such wisdom never could have come from God. Certainly there was no meekness nor modesty in such a bitter spirit. The fountain that sent forth that bitter water was likewise bitter. They might even have been on the side of a righteous course; but win or lose, envying and strife are carnal weapons. Gaining selfish ends is no victory in God's cause. A spirit of competition and rivalry produces nothing in which to glory. We have seen party factions in local churches divided over some issue. By some clever move a majority may score a "victory" and boast in their accomplishment, but such boasting is a lie against the truth. We must guard against our motives to make certain there is no self-seeking, no bitter rivalry. Any claim to success if the motives are not pure is a false claim. No believer ever helped the cause of our Lord Jesus Christ except in a Christian spirit.

We are not to interpret the words in verse 14 as speaking against controversy on spiritual matters. Elsewhere we are exhorted to "earnestly contend for the faith" (Jude 3), "striving together for the faith of the gospel" (Phil. 1:27), and to "hold fast the form of sound words" (2 Tim. 1:13); but let our zeal for the truth be not an unspiritual zeal. In every controversy the truth must be spoken in love (Eph. 4:15), and wherever love prevails the spirit of bitterness cannot enter in.

Worldly wisdom is identified as being "earthly." The believer has been born "from above" and is bound for above; hence he is not to adopt the methods of unbelievers. Worldly-wise men are they "who mind earthly things" (Phil. 3:19); Christians "seek those things which are above" (Col. 3:1).

Then, again, the wisdom of this world is described as "sensual." The margin translates it "natural" in contrast to that which is spiritual (1 Cor. 2:14, 15). The unregenerate man at his best is governed by his own lusts and is described by Jude as "sensual, having not the Spirit" (Jude 19). The wisdom that is earthly and sensual has as its aim the glory of man. Whenever a Christian employs worldly tactics it can only lead him into difficulty. False wisdom belongs to the baser nature in man. It does not come from the Spirit of God.

Finally, verse 15 describes natural wisdom as "devilish" (or demoniacal). The devil, before he became such through pride, was said to be "full of wisdom" (Ezek. 28:12). Satanic wisdom pervades much of man's thinking. James already told us that demons share the faith of true believers. No marvel then that men should share their wisdom. Earthly wisdom finds its origin in Satan, not in God. Charles R. Erdman has written: "It may be employed in discussing religious truth, it may be displayed in defending 'orthodoxy.' " Having heard one heated debate by some "brethren," one might think they were an assembly of demon-possessed men.

"For where envying and strife is, there is confusion and every evil work" (3:16). Such an attitude can only result in commotion and vile practices. Permit worldly wisdom to creep into the assembly of God's people and you have opened the door for every kind of satanic opposition, which is bound to stem the tide of spiritual progress. To be forewarned is to be forearmed. The day that harshness and selfishness enter in among us, we can expect a tide of turbulence. God's wisdom does not allow for confusion, "For God is not the author of confusion, but of peace . . ." (1 Cor. 14:33). Whatever produces tumult and unquietness cannot be from Him. Let us each one pursue an examination of his own heart to discover if he is moved by the motives and methods of the worldy-wise. The lack of genuine modesty may easily open the door for the entrance of Satan into any work for God.

How refreshing to turn from this picture of a wisdom that is "earthly, sensual, devilish," to "the wisdom that is from above" (3:17), from God (1:5). The wisdom that is from above is "first pure." God's wisdom is "pure" in contrast to man's wisdom which is "sensual." You see, when God's Spirit is in control of a man's life his heart is free from every selfish motive. The wisdom of God in control of one's mind makes that one seek only His will. Heavenly wisdom shrinks from selfishness and arrogance. Everything base and everything sensual is abhorred by the Christtian who comes daily to God in prayer asking for wisdom.

Furthermore, the wisdom that is from above is a divine teacher instructing how to live a pure life before God and man. He is a wise Christian who remains free from defilement as he awaits the return of Jesus Christ, for the hope of our Lord's return is a purifying one (1 John 3:3). He is no wise man who fails to shun impure motives and practices. Daniel and his three friends would not defile themselves with the world's meat and drink and religious practices. But why? "As for these four children, God gave them knowledge and skill in all learning and wisdom . . ." (Daniel 1:8, 17). Let a man be guided by the wisdom of the Word of God, and, like Stephen, no one will be able to resist the wisdom by which he speaks (Acts 6:10). An impure person, though wise in the ways of this world, is a fool in God's sight. Any call to seek the wisdom of God is a call to purity. "Keep thyself pure" (1 Tim. 5:22).

The wisdom that is from above is also "peaceable." A truly wise man will seek first *purity* in himself and then *peace* with others. Beware of a false peace that does not come from above, that unholy peace that Satan brings where uncleanness and impurity are allowed to continue. Heavenly wisdom tells the believer to "follow peace with all men" (Heb. 12:14), and "if it be possible, as much as lieth in you, live peaceably with all men" (Rom. 12:18). Purity and peace! What a blessed combination! True righteousness will always pursue peace. Such is wisdom's instruction, teaching all who seek her not to be easily provoked but freed from contentiousness.

Then, too, heaven's wisdom is "gentle"—not harsh or critical, but forbearing and considerate of others. Such wisdom in action, allowing for the ignorance and limitations of others, is beautiful to behold. It is a rare sight but most welcome in these days, when we see one who does not insist upon his rights according to man's laws, but who "guides himself by the broad principles of equity in the sight of God." Too few of us are ready to suffer wrong. How unwise to press our rights!

James continues with his description of the wisdom of God— "Easy to be intreated." It is not easy to admit we might be wrong. Only heavenly wisdom is easily persuaded to make a change. The worldly-wise man is headstrong and obstinate, unwilling to submit to the suggestion of another. Contrariwise, the believer is easy to approach with a change or a suggestion.

Then again, true wisdom is "full of mercy and good fruits, without partiality, and without hypocrisy." What a difference wisdom from above makes in one's life! It pours out itself in compassion, pleads with sinners, and pities the suffering. It is no chameleon, changing color with every surrounding situation in which it finds itself, but always dependably consistent, honest, and sincere.

In the matter of wisdom, the law of sowing and reaping works as in every other realm. He who sows peace will reap peace. "And the fruit of righteousness is sown in peace of them that make peace" (3:18). If we sow arrogance and contention, we must reap the same. Make no mistake about our reaping the evil results of false wisdom. "The wrath of man worketh not the righteousness of God" (1:20). The call is not merely for peace-loving but for peace-making. "Blessed are the peacemakers: for they shall be called the children of God" (Matt. 5:9). The wise Christian does not strive, but seeks by consistent example and teaching to promote peace and good will among the brethren. His success is the fruit of right living. Remember, whatever we sow we reap (Gal. 6:7). Sow peace, and you reap peace. Sow the seed of trouble among Christians, and you are in for trouble. Only those who sow the good seed can expect to reap a good harvest. Be wise.

Look all around you, find some one in need,
Help somebody today!
Tho' it be little—a neighborly deed—
Help somebody today!

Many are waiting a kind, loving word,
Help somebody today!
Thou hast a message, O let it be heard,
Help somebody today!

Many have burdens too heavy to bear,
Help somebody today!
Grief is the portion of some everywhere,
Help somebody today!

Some are discouraged and weary in heart,
Help somebody today!
Someone the journey to heaven should start,
Help somebody today!

Help somebody today,
Somebody along life's way;
Let sorrow be ended,
The friendless befriended,
Oh, help somebody today!

STRIFE THROUGH
SELFISHNESS

James 4:1-6

1. From whence come wars and fightings among you? come they not hence, even of your lusts that war in your members?

2. Ye lust, and have not: ye kill, and desire to have, and cannot obtain: ye fight and war, yet ye have not, because ye ask not.

3. Ye ask, and receive not, because ye ask amiss, that ye may consume it upon your lusts.

4. Ye adulterers and adulteresses, know ye not that the friendship of the world is enmity with God? whosoever therefore will be a friend of the world is the enemy of God.

5. Do ye think that the scripture saith in vain, The spirit that dwelleth in us lusteth to envy?

6. But he giveth more grace. Wherefore he saith, God resisteth the proud, but giveth grace unto the humble.

How striking the contrast between the closing words of the preceding chapter and the beginning of Chapter Four! There we saw the fruits of righteousness being sown in peace; here we are brought face to face with wars and fightings among believers. "You" in verse one refers to the "brethren" of the dispersion to whom our Apostle has been addressing himself throughout, those brethren out of whose mouth proceeded both blessing and cursing (3:10). At times the saints in the early church showed deep affection for each other, but they had their moments of bitter strife also. Paul spoke freely against "envying, and strife, and divisions" (1 Cor. 3:3). Said he: "For I fear . . . lest there be debates, envyings, wraths, strifes, backbitings, whisperings, swellings, tumults" (2 Cor. 12:20). The atmosphere in which believers live is potentially one of strife.

James discloses the cause of unrest. This is a logical approach to the problem since proper diagnosis is a necessary prerequisite to cure. Nations, churches, families and individuals could profit much from a study of these verses. Extirpate the cause of wars and fightings and you have settled the disposition of this evil monstrosity.

James answers the question in the form of another question. "Come they not hence, even of your lusts that war in your members?" There is the source. Strife springs up in men's hearts in the longings and lusts within. All our attempts to justify ourselves are rooted in the lust for prominence, power, or possessions. An honest look at the matter will concede that selfish passions are the cause of strife. Nieboer writes: "So the real trouble was self-pleasing and self-love. Herod got into trouble because of the love of pleasure (Mark 6:14-29); Judas, because of the love of money (Mark 14:10, 11); Hezekiah, because of the love of display (2 Kings 20:12-18); Adoni-bezek, because of the love of power (Judges 1:5-7); and Diotrophes, because of the love of pre-eminence (3 John 9, 10)." Our Lord said, and we repeat it here for emphasis: "For from within, out of the heart of men, proceed evil thoughts, adulteries, fornications, murders, Thefts, covetousness, wickedness, deceit, lasciviousness, an evil eye, blasphemy, pride, foolishness: All these evil things come from within, and defile the man" (Mark 7:21-23).

James did not argue for the existence of strife; he assumed it. Neither did he give his readers an opportunity to blame their quarrelsome spirit on environment beyond their control; he tore away the veil of every imaginary possibility and showed that their own greedy hearts were the real cause of their strife. Selfishness is at all times destructive of peace. True, believers may sit week by week under the ministry of God's Word and like the hearer in the parable of our Lord, never bring forth the fruit of peace because the Word is choked by the cares of this world and the deceitfulness of riches (Matt. 13:22). Wherever lusts and pleasures rule the heart, conflicts and disputes will continue. A dissatisfied heart is never at peace with God or man.

The conflict, says the Apostle, is "in your members," the lusts creating the conflict being part of the Old Nature. "The old man, which is corrupt according to the deceitful lusts" is at war with "the new man, which after God is created in righteousness and true holiness" (Eph. 4:22, 24). In writing to the Galatians, Paul speaks of this same war with different words: "For the flesh lusteth against the Spirit, and the Spirit against the flesh: and these are contrary the one to the other: so that ye cannot do the things that ye would" (Gal. 5:17). If we yield our members as instruments of unrighteousness unto sin instead of yielding ourselves unto God (Rom. 6:13), there will be unrest and turbulence within and without; hence the exhortation to "present your bodies a living sacrifice, holy, acceptable unto God . . ." (Rom. 12:1). In our day an insatiable thirst for pleasure is destroying our thirst for the things of God, and these sinful, selfish gratifications are responsible for the strife among Christians, all the while warring against the soul (1 Pet. 2:11). Desires of a good sort are commendable, but desires after the gratification of the flesh and the world disturb the peace of your life as well as the lives of others.

What does our selfishness and covetousness get us? Verse two says: "Ye lust, and *have not:* ye kill, and desire to have, and *cannot obtain:* ye fight and war, yet ye *have not,* because ye ask not" (4:2). Pay particular attention to the words, *"have not . . . cannot obtain . . . have not."* If this verse tells us anything at all, it thrice reminds us that the natural heart of man is never contented. The awful craving for the pleasures, the privileges, and the pre-eminence in mundane things, fills us with jealousy and envy, which in turn produces an unholy restlessness with inevitable confusion and strife. Satisfaction in the things of this world is like a mirage, seemingly within our reach, but always eluding us, leaving us fretful and fighting like spoiled children. We all have passed through these experiences and we admit that under the sun all is vanity and vexation of spirit. "Ye lust . . . ye kill . . . ye fight . . . ye ask," and all to satisfy the lustings of the flesh which never can be satisfied. Our Lord said: "Whosoever drinketh of this water shall thirst again" (John 4:13). The natural heart is always thirsting. If a man gets power, he craves more power. If he gets money, he wants more money. If he enjoys a season of sinful pleasure, he seeks more of the same. And so it goes! When one's body, mind, and spirit are not fully yielded to God, life becomes one vicious circle of seeking but never satisfying. Oh, my reader, can't you see that the desire for the wrong things, prompted by wrong motives at work in our members, wages ceaseless warfare against everything and everyone that stand in the way of their gratification? And when we get what we thought we wanted, we are left still empty, unsatisfied, and seeking! "Ye . . . cannot obtain."

Observe how closely related this problem is to our prayer life. "Ye have not, because ye ask not. Ye ask, and receive not, because ye ask amiss, that ye may consume it upon your lusts" (or pleasure) (4:2, 3). Here we are shown just why we "have not" real satisfaction of soul. There are *two* reasons given. *First,* prayerlessness. "Ye ask not." We failed to make our desires a matter of prayer. Our heavenly Father gives liberally to those who ask of Him (1:5, 6, 17). "Ask, and it shall be given you; seek, and ye shall find; knock, and it shall be opened unto you: For every one that asketh receiveth; and he that seeketh findeth; and to him that knocketh it shall be opened" (Matt. 7:7, 8). Examine your prayer life, and I believe you will agree with God's Word that one reason we do not get things *from* God is that we do not ask things *of* God. I said prayers for many years before I could lay claim to having received one thing as a direct answer to my prayers. Not all prayer is petition, but certainly all who read the Scriptures know that asking is an essential part of one's prayer life. When we do not make our desires the subject of selfless, sincere, earnest prayer, we cannot hope to be satisfied. Indeed prayer is the secret to peace and contentment.

Paul adds to the message of James: "Be careful for nothing; but in every thing by prayer and supplication with thanksgiving let your requests be made known unto God. And the peace of God, which passeth all understanding, shall keep your hearts and minds through Christ Jesus" (Phil. 4:6, 7). The Christian who walks in unbroken prayer fellowship with his Lord is content in whatsoever state he finds himself (Phil. 4:11). Where Christians depend upon God, the restlessness and discontent that generate strife are absent. Learn to trust your heavenly Father not only in spiritual matters that affect your eternal well-being but for all temporal needs amidst the cares of this world. We can depend upon Him for the life to come and for the present as well.

The *second* reason given for the discontent that engenders strife is in verse 3: "Ye ask, and receive not, because ye ask amiss, that ye may consume it upon your lusts" (4:3). This verse answers the objection which says: "I prayed and asked, but God did not give me what I prayed for." Possibly the reason for your prayer going unanswered lies right here. Many times we do not get what we ask for simply because we ask selfishly that we might use the things for which we ask on our own pleasures. There is such a thing as praying in the will of God. "And this is the confidence that we have in Him, that, if we ask any thing according to His will, He heareth us" (1 John 5:14). A wise father or mother will not give a little child something harmful just because he begs for it. When we pray for things which God knows will harm us, He purposely, out of love, withholds them. Why not thank Him that He never permits His children to make Him chargeable for their own lustful pleasures? We earthly parents are sometimes guilty of so injuring our children, but God never!

If whatever we ask from God we are willing to dedicate to Him, we may be certain that He will answer. "But seek ye first the kingdom of God, and His righteousness; and all these things shall be added unto you" (Matt. 6:33). I once heard of a brother in Christ who, when asking for anything in prayer, sincerely told God why he wanted it and how he intended to use it. This practice doubtless kept him from requesting things to satisfy the desires of his old nature. Even our Lord Jesus prayed: "not as I will, but as Thou wilt" (Matt. 26:39). I am sure we shall be eternally thankful in heaven for our unanswered prayers, but while we pass through this earthly experience, let us not pervert the true Biblical practice of prayer by asking for those things that pander to our fleshly desires.

When a Christian learns the Biblical rules of prayer, he will not unwittingly abuse its privileges nor belabor the ears of God. When we ask according to His will, we ask unselfishly in moderation for His glory. "Not I, but Christ" (Gal. 2:20) ought to be the passion of every child of God and Paul's principle should underlie every desire— "Whether therefore ye eat, or drink, or whatsoever ye do, do all to the glory of God" (1 Cor. 10:31).

Would you live at peace with God, with yourself, and with your brethren in Christ? If you would, ask God not for what you want but only for those things He wants you to have; not for what you want to do, but for enablement to do that which He would have you do.

The causes for strife and unrest continue in verse 4. "Ye adulterers and adulteresses, know ye not that the friendship of the world is enmity with God? whosoever therefore will be a friend of the world is the enemy of God" (4:4). Worldliness in a Christian's life must of necessity create disturbance and turmoil because neutrality is impossible where you have a divided allegiance. Can an unfaithful husband hope for harmony in his home, or a disloyal wife peace?

The term "adulterers and adulteresses" is Scriptural language. The unfaithfulness of a believer to the Lord is compared to that of a wife toward her husband. When Israel fell into idolatry or worldliness, she was called the adulterous wife of Jehovah. Speaking of Israel, the prophet writes: ". . . for the land hath committed great whoredom, departing from the Lord" (Hosea 1:2). "My people . . . have gone a-whoring from under their God" (Hosea 4:12). Isaiah said: "For thy Maker is thine husband" (Isaiah 54:5). Our Lord used similar language when He referred to unbelieving Jews of His own day, saying: "A wicked and adulterous generation seeketh after a sign . . ." (Matt. 16:4). "Whosoever therefore shall be ashamed of me and of my words in this adulterous and sinful generation; of him also shall the Son of man be ashamed, when He cometh in the glory of His Father with the holy angels" (Mark 8:38).

The relationship of the Christian to the Lord Jesus Christ is explained in marital language in the New Testament. Our Saviour's love for us is likened unto that of a loyal, loving groom for his bride. "Husbands, love your wives, even as Christ also loved the church, and gave Himself for it" (Eph. 5:25). Christians are as chaste virgins espoused to Jesus Christ (2 Cor. 11:2), waiting the consummation of the marriage at Christ's return (Rev. 19:7). But, alas, James exposes the unfaithfulness on the part of some Christians, charging them with spiritual adultery similar to that of Old Testament believers, namely, idolatry and worldliness. The Christian who turns from Christ and His Church to seek pleasure and satisfaction at the cisterns of this world are like unfaithful women who leave their husbands to seek sensual pleasure with other men. God is jealous over us with a holy jealousy. He purchased us at great sacrifice to Himself; hence He wants us solely for Himself.

Just what form does spiritual adultery or worldliness assume? The "world" of which James warns is not the world of created things or what some might refer to as the world of nature. Our planet and all that God put on it in creation is to be admired as the work of His hands. Neither is James suggesting that we are to withdraw from the world of humanity. God loves the world of mankind and we are expected to love it too. James has in mind this world-system and scheme of things which runs contrary to the plain teaching of God's Word. This present world-system, or present age, has Satan as its "god" (2 Cor. 4:4) and "prince" (John 14:30); hence it is declared "evil" (Gal. 1:4). "The whole world lieth in wickedness" (1 John 5:19), hating Christ and all who follow Him (John 15:18, 19). In its entirety, the system that rejects Jesus Christ and His teaching can occupy no rightful place in a Christian's life.

It is in a deep exercise of my own soul that I speak frankly to you about worldliness. Face the facts with me! The adultery of the Church to her Lord is worldliness. I am not now thinking of those things frowned upon by most Christians, as drinking alcoholic beverages, gambling, smoking, sex, show business, and the like. Rather does my mind go out to those things which make up "the world" of most believers in Christ, things which are not harmful in themselves, but which come between your own soul and your fellowship with God in prayer and the study of the Holy Scriptures. There are those who confess Christ as Saviour and who, like Demas, forsake the Saviour and the saints "having loved this present world" (2 Tim. 4:10), or who, like Peter, follow "afar off" (Luke 22:54). When Jesus calls men to follow Him He does not expect them to turn back ever. But alas! Some of you who one day made a decision to follow the Son of God could not resist the after appeal of the world. You went back, didn't you? Your business, your house, your automobile, or something else, took your affections, and your Saviour was crowded out. Such is worldliness.

It is impossible to walk in spiritual fellowship with God, at the same time following the world. "Love not the world, neither the things that are in the world. If any man love the world, the love of the Father is not in him. For all that is in the world, the lust of the flesh, and the lust of the eyes, and the pride of life, is not of the Father, but is of the world. And the world passeth away, and the lust thereof: but he that doeth the will of God abideth for ever" (1 John 2:15-17). He who corrupts himself with the vanities of this world cannot truthfully say he loves God. God and this world are rivals for the allegiance of your heart and mine; and whenever a Christian becomes a friend of the world, he breaks his marriage vows to God. "Whosoever therefore will be a friend of the world is the enemy of God."

Exactly who has our fondest affection? Is it God or the world?

With weeping, Paul reminded the brethren at Philippi that among them were "enemies of the cross of Christ . . . who mind earthly things" (Phil. 3:17-19). Minding earthly things, earthly possessions, earthly pleasures, earthly recognition, is worldly. "Set your affection on things above, not on things on the earth" (Col. 3:2). Charles Brown draws our attention to that grand old hymn of Isaac Watts, "Am I a Soldier of the Cross?" In the third stanza he raises the question of our relation to this world,

> "Is this vile world a friend to grace,
>   To help me on to God?"

I feel certain that every Bible-believing child of God can answer the question of this hymn with an emphatic "No."

James continues the question method by asking another: "Do ye think that the scripture saith in vain, The Spirit that dwelleth in us lusteth to envy?" (4:5). The exact meaning of this verse seems a bit difficult. Personally, I have been unable to find this quotation, or its equivalent, anywhere in the Bible. However, there is an obvious application for each of us, but first, let us seek to get the sense of the words, "The Spirit that dwelleth in us lusteth to envy." We might paraphrase this to read as follows: "The Spirit, who hath taken up His abode in us, enviously yearns over us." I have capitalized the word Spirit, for I believe James is referring to the Holy Spirit. The Holy Spirit, indwelling us, is longing after something: namely, to make us wholly Christ's, to bring us to the place where we have no divided allegiance. The Holy Spirit has just one envy, one desire, one longing; that is, our entire devotion to Jesus Christ. God warned His people of old time to have no other gods, neither to bow down to them, for, said He: "I the Lord thy God am a jealous God" (Deut. 5:1-9). This is the intense desire of divine love, and the dispensations do not alter it. God's pure and perfect love for us yearns over us, for He too longs to be loved by His own. This is the consistent teaching of all Scripture, and it is not mere vain (or empty) teaching. No teaching in the Word of God can be labeled meaningless.

Pay close ettention to this verse, my friend. The warnings of Scripture are not empty words. To see the wrangling and worldliness among some Christains, one might conclude the Bible to be a book of empty phrases; but such is not the case. In Old Testament times Israel learned the hard way that God is not mocked. The scattering and sufferings of the Jewish people stand as a solemn warning to God's people everywhere that the Scriptures do not speak in vain. Whenever a child of God sets his affection on anything in this world, thereby relegating Jesus Christ to a secondary place in his heart, he is in for serious trouble. "For he that soweth to his flesh shall of the flesh reap corruption . . ." (Gal. 6:8). Do not tamper with God's laws.

But bless His holy name, our heavenly Father has a sure cure for our ills: *"He giveth more grace . . ."* It is by "grace" we are saved (Eph. 2:8), and by "more grace" we are sustained. God showed grace at Calvary in the salvation of hell-deserving sinners. Now He stands ready to give more grace in welcoming back to His fellowship His straying children. Thank God divine grace did not cease to flow toward us when we received Jesus Christ as Saviour, else where would we be at the present?

Now note carefully please who it is that receives the privileges of "more grace." Certainly it is not to the proud, for pride in a believer's heart keeps him at a distance from God. Whenever pride keeps us from confessing our faults, God "resists" us: that is, He puts us away from Himself. Let us never minimize our part as Christians in living a separated life. The needed grace to triumph over our fears and our foes is never given when we refuse to bow in contrition, confession, and humble submission before God. "Though the Lord be high, yet hath He respect unto the lowly: but the proud He knoweth afar off" (Psalm 138:6). "Surely He scorneth the scorners: but He giveth grace unto the lowly" (Proverbs 3:34). Do not presume upon His grace, dear ones, for He will only resist you. Only as we surrender to those longings and yearnings of divine love, do we become the recipients of "more grace." ". . . Be subject one to another, and be clothed with humility: for God resisteth the proud, and giveth grace to the humble" (1 Peter 5:5).

"Let us therefore come boldly unto the throne of grace, that we may obtain mercy, and find grace to help in time of need" (Heb. 4:16).

My glorious Victor, Prince Divine,
Clasp these surrendered hands in Thine;
At length my will is all Thine own,
Glad vassal of a Saviour's throne.

My Master, lead me to Thy door;
Pierce this now willing ear once more;
Thy bonds are freedom; let me stay
With Thee, to toil, endure, obey.

Yes, ear and hand, and thought and will,
Use all in Thy dear slavery still!
Self's weary liberties I cast
Beneath Thy feet; there keep them fast.

Tread them still down; and then I know,
These hands shall with Thy gifts o'erflow;
And pierced ears shall hear the tone
Which tells me Thou and I are one.

SECURITY THROUGH
SUBMISSION

James 4:7-10

7. Submit yourselves therefore to God. Resist the devil, and he will flee from you.

8. Draw nigh to God, and he will draw nigh to you. Cleanse your hands, ye sinners; and purify your hearts, ye double minded.

9. Be afflicted, and mourn, and weep: let your laughter be turn to mourning, and your joy to heaviness.

10. Humble yourselves in the sight of the Lord, and he shall lift you up.

"Submit yourselves therefore to God. Resist the devil, and he will flee from you" (4:7). This is one of the most positive neglected formulas offered to Christians. It tells us why so many fail to resist the devil. The first step that every backslider must take is submission to his heavenly Father. Never try to withstand the enemy in human submission. No matter what it might be that has defeated you, if you "humble yourselves in the sight of the Lord, He shall lift you up" (verse 10). No hope nor help is available for one caught in the grip of worldliness, refusing to renounce self-will and to take God's will as his own. There must needs be submission both to divine love and divine law.

Then we are told to "resist the devil." This combination of *submitting* and *resisting* leads to conquest in battle. Humbly submit to the divine Captain and courageously stand against the enemy. If this plan is carried out, James says that the devil "will flee from you." Whatever you do, never resist God and submit to the devil. Those who have erred in this respect know full well what a tragic and costly mistake was theirs. Our Lord was the greatest example of submission to the Father's will (Matt.

26:39), and in the hour when Satan attacked Him He was able
to resist the foe so that the devil fled from Him (Matt. 4:11).
The devil is powerful, but if we resist him, according to the
Scripture, he will be put to flight. Coupled with submission to
God is the blessed companion truth of drawing nigh to God.
"Draw nigh to God, and He will draw nigh to you . . ." (4:8).
James has just been showing us that the only way to resist evil
and the Evil One is to submit to God. Here he adds that if we
do this, God will come to rescue us in our need. What happened
in our Lord's wilderness temptation when Satan attacked Him?
He submitted to the Father's Word, and not only did Satan flee
from Him, but in the very same verse we read that "angels came
and ministered unto Him" (Matt. 4:11). He drew nigh to the
Father, and the Father in turn drew nigh to Him.

Real comfort and courage come to every child of God who experiences His nearness, and it seems to me that the heart of the
average man cries out with Job: "Oh that I knew where I might
find Him!" (Job 23:3). Many persons facing complex problems
yearn for God's nearness. On this hunger many psychiatric
quacks are getting rich. Even some Protestant clergymen have
resorted to operating clinics where sentimental and emaciated
peace of mind gimmicks are offered to resolve inner tension and
restlessness. The quiet mood of "positive thinking" is negative
compared with what the Bible teaches.

The nearness to God here promised is available to every child
of God meeting divine requirements for it. Most expositors hold
prayer to be the most prominent element in our drawing near to
God. Personally, I feel safer if I commence with the Word of God
and then pray according to the Scriptures. We have already indicated that prayers offered contrary to the plain teaching of the
Bible remain unanswered, for the heart must be right as a condition to effective prayer. The greatest privilege ever afforded
the sinful human race is to draw nigh to God. When we think of
God's majesty and might and holiness, we stand in awe that He
would allow us to come near to Him.

Permit this word first to any reader of these pages who is unsaved, still in sin, and far from God. There is only one way possible for a sinner to draw nigh to God. First, you must confess you are a sinner, "For all have sinned, and come short of the glory of God" (Rom. 3:23). Second, you must believe that God in love sent His Son Jesus Christ to die in your place and for your sins, for "God commendeth His love toward us, in that, while we were yet sinners, Christ died for us" (Rom. 5:8). Third, you must come to God in prayer and tell Him you are a sinner and that you are confessing Christ as your personal Saviour, for "if thou shalt confess with thy mouth the Lord Jesus, and shalt believe in thine heart that God hath raised Him from the dead, thou shalt be saved" (Rom. 10:9).

Apart from Christ's substitutionary death, no sinner can get near to God. "But now in Christ Jesus ye who sometimes were far off are made nigh by the blood of Christ" (Eph. 2:13). "Having therefore, brethren, boldness to enter into the holiest by the blood of Jesus" (Heb. 10:19). When our Lord died on the Cross, the veil in the temple was rent in twain from the top to the bottom, thus signifying that Christ, in His death, made it possible for any believing sinner to come to God (Matt. 27:51). In Old Testament times only the priests who offered sacrifices and ministered in the temple could "draw near," but now all believers are priests and can come into the closest possible relationship to God. "For the law made nothing perfect, but the bringing in of a better hope did; by the which we draw nigh unto God" (Heb. 7:19). By placing implicit trust in God's Son you can draw nigh even as He is nigh.

> "Near to the heart of God,
> Nearer I cannot be,
> For in the Person of His Son
> I'm just as near as He."

But let us return to our text to seek its application for the Christian, for James is writing, you recall, to believers. David said, "It is good for me to draw near to God" (Psalm 73:28). Yes, and it is good for us too. In His presence there is peace and joy. Since He invites us to draw near (Heb. 10:22), we injure ourselves and grieve Him when we fail.

How must we draw nigh to God as Christians? There is a sure approach to Him. James adds: "Cleanse your hands . . . and purify your hearts" (4:8). Clean hands and pure hearts are a necessary preparation for any Christian coming to God. The Psalmist asked: "Who shall ascend into the hill of the Lord? or who shall stand in His holy place?" Then the answer: "He that hath clean hands, and a pure heart; who hath not lifted up his soul unto vanity, nor sworn deceitfully" (Psalm 24:3, 4). My Christian friends, James is speaking to us, as well as to the Christians of his own day, and he calls us "sinners" and "double minded" men and women. Too often we give way to the soft sentimental jargon that winks at the sins of saints. You and I need God's presence in these days, and the need will increase with the passing of time; but we cannot expect God to draw nigh to us if we fail to draw nigh to Him, and we cannot draw nigh to Him with soiled hands and stained hearts. All hypocrisy and double-mindedness must be put aside.

This is the second time James speaks of the "double-minded" man. In Chapter One, verse 8, the double-minded man is said to be unstable in all his ways. He is that man whose affection is divided, who expresses love for God on one occasion and then turns about face to love this world. Such a one who has not ceased from all divided allegiance and separated himself from all sinful alliances cannot enjoy God's nearness.

Fellowship with God is never found in the mere saying of prayers. Many persons who say prayers, some who recite the so-called Lord's prayer religiously, are not saved at all. Mere formal saying of prayers will never bring God near to any man. We need the outward cleansing suggested by the expression "clean hands" and the inward purification set forth in the words "purify your hearts." It is wrong to attempt to pray without first confessing our sins to God. "I will therefore that men pray every where, lifting up holy hands, without wrath and doubting" (1 Tim. 2:8). "If I regard iniquity in my heart, the Lord will not hear me" (Psalm 66:18). "Let us draw near with a true heart in full assurance of faith, having our hearts sprinkled from an evil conscience, and our bodies washed with pure water" (Heb. 10:22). The first step toward God, and the only one that will bring God nigh unto us, is the consciousness and confession of inner depravity.

James is calling for practical holiness among Christians. He is pleading for the surrender of our hearts and our bodies as a necessary requisite to communion with God. In this he is but reflecting the teaching of our Lord Jesus Christ, who said to the religious sinners and the double-minded of His day, "Ye hypocrites, well did Esaias prophesy of you, saying, This people draweth nigh unto Me with their mouth, and honoureth Me with their lips; but their heart is far from Me. But in vain they do worship Me, teaching for doctrines the commandments of men" (Matt. 15:7-9). God will meet any of us half way, but the first step is one of repentance and confession. If we refuse to come to Him, it must be said of us as it was written of God's ancient people, "Behold, the Lord's hand is not shortened, that it cannot save; neither His ear heavy, that it cannot hear: But your iniquities have separated between you and your God, and your sins have hid His face from you, that He will not hear" (Isaiah 59:1, 2).

The remedy for insecurity continues: "Be afflicted, and mourn, and weep: let your laughter be turned to mourning, and your joy to heaviness" (4:9). A strange request, this! But here is heavenly wisdom. How contrary to the wisdom of this world! These words of James constitute a direct call for genuine repentance. When a man sees his own sinful heart, he can hardly shout for joy but rather will cry as did Paul: "O wretched man that I am" (Rom. 7:24)!

The "laughter" here is not that superficial cover-over smile that was popularized during World War I: "Pack up your troubles in your old kit bag and smile, smile, smile." That smile will not work, for there is nothing to work it. Such a superficial prescription holds no security. Our Lord said: "Blessed are they that mourn: for they shall be comforted" (Matt. 5:4). The chastening of our own hearts because of our sin is not provocative of careless laughter. Mourning and heaviness always accompany a deep sense of sin. The Bible is the most joyful Book in the world, and Christianity the most joyful religion, but the real abiding joy of the cleansed and forgiven sinner can come only after deep sorrow for sin. Fellow believers, we must keep our hearts and bodies pure. Whenever you fall into sin, repent with godly sorrow and humbly confess your sin to God. None but fools make sport of sin (Prov. 10:23) in the light of the wages of sin. Learn to mourn for your sins, my brothers and sisters in Christ. Shake off the deadly indifference that mocks at this dread enemy of your souls. "For if we would judge ourselves we should not be judged" (1 Cor. 11:31).

Finally, "Humble yourselves in the sight of the Lord, and He shall lift you up" (4:10). This summarizes James's introductory command. "Submit yourselves . . . Humble yourselves." This indeed is the secret to the security that brings peace and joy. This blessing cannot accompany a false cloak of humility. Trying to act and talk humbly before men bespeaks pride at its worst. It must be *"in the sight of the Lord."* Do you see your own heart for what it is? God sees it too, only His eyes are as a flame of fire piercing the innermost recesses of our very thoughts.

Again James reflects upon the teachings of Christ, where He said: "And whosoever shall exalt himself shall be abased; and he that shall humble himself shall be exalted" (Matt. 23:12). Self-exaltation is the breakdown of our civilization, the ruining factor in many a man's ministry, and the cause of much frustration and insecurity. He who must be on top of the ladder of success to feel secure has a proud estimate of his own importance. The bootstrap method of lifting up one's self must always end with a hard letdown. The way up is first down. "Humble yourselves therefore under the mighty hand of God, that He may exalt you in due time" (1 Peter 5:6).

Our verse concludes with the words "He shall lift you up." If we allow God to lift us up, no man will be able to withstand our exalted position. As we humble ourselves before the Lord, He will lift us out of any circumstance whether it be temptation, sin, or despair. No man ever yet took a humble position before the Lord without seeing God lift him up. There have been many Biblical examples of self-abasement and divine exaltation, but our Lord Jesus Christ is the greatest example of all. "He humbled Himself, and became obedient unto death, even the death of the cross. Wherefore God also hath highly exalted Him and given Him a name which is above every name" (Phil. 2:8, 9).

Have we come to the end of ourselves? When we do, God will be there extending the divine hand to lift us up. Do we seek a true elevation? Let us cast ourselves down under a sense of our infirmity, and God will raise us to heights where pride can never come.

If all that we say in a single day,
    With never a word left out,
Were printed each night in clear black and white
    'Twould prove queer reading, no doubt.
And then just suppose, ere our eyes we could close
    We must read the whole record through;
Then wouldn't we sigh, and wouldn't we try
    A great deal less talking to do?
And I more than half think
That many a kink
Would be smoother in life's tangled thread
If half that we say in a single day were left forever unsaid.

BACKSLIDING THROUGH
BACKBITING

James 4:11-12

11. Speak not evil one of another, brethren. He that speaketh evil of his brother, and judgeth his brother, speaketh evil of the law, and judgeth the law: but if thou judge the law, thou art not a doer of the law, but a judge.

12. There is one lawgiver, who is able to save and to destroy: who art thou that judgest another?

The weighty subject matter in verses eleven and twelve demands our careful attention. Had I announced my subject in the newspaper I would not be looking for an overflow crowd. This text is not the spectacular type. In this day of light and frivolous thinking, too many among us engage in forbidden sins for our pastime. One such forbidden practice is the subject of the verses before us, hence its lack of appeal. Somehow Christians do not delight in listening to a Bible exposition which speaks against their favorite diversion.

"Speak not evil one of another, brethren . . ." The topic is not a new one for James. Already he has urged his readers to be "slow to speak" (1:19) and to bridle the tongue (1:26). Then, throughout the third chapter he dwells on the right and wrong use of the tongue. Now again in our present chapter he takes up this sin of the saints: namely, speaking evil of others.

The New Testament Greek word *Katalaleo* is translated "backbiter," and it means *one who speaks against another*. I find it at least two times in the New Testament; where it is used of unbelievers (Rom. 1:30), and also of believers (2 Cor. 12:20). The sin of speaking against others is common among unsaved persons, and obviously it clings to some even after they become saved.

Regarding this sin James addresses himself to the "brethren," for it is a grievous wrong when one Christian speaks against another. Speaking evil of others may take on one of several forms. The worst of all types of evil speaking is the downright untruth. God made it plain in His dealings with Israel that no man should speak falsely of another. "Thou shalt not bear false witness against thy neighbour" (Exod. 20:16). Lying originated with the devil, for our Lord said: "When he speaketh a lie, he speaketh of his own: for he is a liar, and the father of it" (John 8:44). I doubt if there is a more diabolical use of speech than this. It was a lie that Satan used to cause the fall in Eden (Gen. 3:4). He dared to tell Eve that what God said was not so. He filled the hearts of Ananias and Sapphira to lie about the disposition of their money (Acts 5:3). Christians are warned to lie not one to another since it is one of the deeds of the old man (Col. 3:9). Our daily prayer should be like that of the Psalmist: "Remove from me the way of lying" (Psalm 119:29). In no way does one prove himself a follower of Satan more than when he deliberately propagates a lie. Let us not be guilty of exaggerating or distorting the truth ever.

Another form of evil speaking rears its ugly head when we spread information containing the faults and sins of others, even though the information be true. The teaching of the Scriptures interposes a prohibition on telling abroad the sins and weaknesses of our brethren in Christ. Peter writes that "love shall cover the multitude of sins" (1 Peter 4:8, A.S.V.). It was to His own people that God said: "Thou shalt not go up and down as a talebearer among thy people" (Lev. 19:16). Not only must we refrain from backbiting but likewise discourage it by turning a deaf ear. A proverb says: "The north wind driveth away rain: so doth an angry countenance a backbiting tongue" (Prov. 25:23). Giving ear to the backbiter only encourages him in his evil way. Never receive such a one with favor.

Let a Christian examine his motives for speaking evil against his brother, and they will be found the product of his own evil heart, rooted in vanity, envy, jealousy, or self-seeking. The very thought of another Christian prospering causes some Christians to create a build-up for themselves and so they speak disparagingly or slanderously of the one prospered.

James proceeds to state what the wrong is in speaking evil of another. "He that speaketh evil of his brother, and judgeth his brother, speaketh evil of the law, and judgeth the law" (4:11). The *law* here is doubtless the royal law of love. Of this James spoke in Chapter Two (verse 8). When one fails to heed the law, any law, he is judging the law to be of no value or importance. When we obey the law we recognize its righteousness and divine sovereignty over us, but when we willfully violate it, we actually condemn it. Any breach of a law is an actual repudiation of the law. If I condemn a brother when God's laws forbid it, I usurp the role of a judge, and in so doing I become a violator myself. The Scriptures are clear on this.

Jesus said: "Judge not, that ye be not judged. For with what judgment ye judge, ye shall be judged: and with what measure ye mete, it shall be measured to you again. And why beholdest thou the mote that is in thy brother's eye, but considerest not the beam that is in thine own eye? Or how wilt thou say to thy brother, Let me pull out the mote out of thine eye; and behold, a beam is in thine own eye? Thou hypocrite, first cast out the beam out of thine own eye; and then shalt thou see clearly to cast out the mote out of thy brother's eye" (Matt. 7:1-5). Here Christ is telling His hearers that no man is faultless; therefore the place to commence judging is one's self. The law governing relationships between men is the law, "Thou shalt love thy neighbour as thyself." When we obey the royal law of love, we are not a law unto ourselves.

James continues: *"but if thou judge the law, thou art not a doer of the law, but a judge."* There is no Scripture to allow one individual to judge another. The Word of God says: "For the Father judgeth no man, but hath committed all judgment unto the Son" (John 5:22). The Father has reserved the judgment seat for the Son. That seat is called the judgment seat of Christ (Rom. 14:10; 2 Cor. 5:10). It is the judgment seat before which every Christian must stand. You see, beloved, when we take our place on that seat and publish judgment upon others we are out of order, since judgment of this kind has never been entrusted to any of us. Let us pray God daily that we might not be guilty of trespassing that divine and sacred task which is reserved for our Lord Jesus Christ.

At this point, permit me to add a word or two from the pen of the Apostle Paul. "Therefore thou art inexcusable, O man, whosoever thou art that judgest: for wherein thou judgest another, thou condemnest thyself; for thou that judgest doest the same things" (Rom. 2:1). We cannot mistake the plain teaching of this verse. When we judge others, it is usually true that we ourselves are guilty, if not of the same failings of the one we judged, or failings of a different sort which could be worse. Since we are not perfect, we cannot judge with accuracy our fellowmen. The text leaves us without excuse.

Paul speaks again on our subject. "Let not him that eateth despise him that eateth not; and let not him which eateth not judge him that eateth: for God hath received him" (Rom. 14:3). The Apostle is here dealing with the matter of individual conscience. Let not the instructed sit in judgment of the untaught nor the untaught, of the instructed. Let not the weak impute narrow-mindedness to the strong, nor vice versa.

Where the Word of God does not regulate certain matters, we are not to regulate another's life in relation to those matters, but do well to be silent also. The context here in Romans 14 deals with the principle of Christian conscience.

I have a dear brother in Christ whom I regard highly in the Lord. My friend is strongly opposed to the use of any pictures in the Lord's work. He will have nothing to do with visual aids of any description. He refuses to allow his wife or children to attend a service where slides or moving pictures are to be shown, even if those pictures were taken by a missionary, sound in the faith, to give people at home a firsthand view of some foreign field. Now, quite frankly, I must place certain limitations on the use of pictures insofar as the showing of those pictures touch the life of the Body of Christ, but I do not go nearly so far in my restrictions as does my brother in Christ. With him I believe it is a matter of conscience; therefore I am not justified in imputing narrow-mindedness or superstition to him. By the same token, my restrictions and liberties in the use of religious films are a matter of conscience also, and he has no right to adopt a critical or censorious attitude toward me or others who do not see eye to eye with him. Let us beware of the danger of unbrotherliness. We are both servants of Jesus Christ, and we stand or fall before Him who is our Lord and Master (Rom. 14:4).

"But why dost thou judge thy brother? or why dost thou set at nought thy brother? for we shall all stand before the judgment seat of Christ" (Rom. 14:10). Again we are reminded that judgment is Christ's divine prerogative, and that no Christian has any right to usurp it in his relationship to other believers. It cannot be denied that most of us do some things that are questionable in the eyes of others; but it would be much more profitable for the whole Body of Christ if we left all matters of judgment to God, for "every one of us shall give account of himself to God" (Rom. 14:12). I will have to do it. Everyone of you, my brothers and sisters in Christ, will have to do it. In view of this Paul adds: "Let us not therefore judge one another any more" (Rom. 14:13).

Returning now to James we read: "There is one lawgiver, who is able to save and to destroy: who art thou that judgest another?" (4:12). God is the giver of His own law, and the only true Judge of those who violate it. Again Paul writes: ". . . He that judgeth me is the Lord. Therefore judge nothing before the time, until the Lord come, who both will bring to light the hidden things of darkness, and will make manifest the counsels of the hearts: and then shall every man have praise of God" (1 Cor. 4:4, 5). No one can alter His laws or argue His decisions, since He alone can determine the destiny of man's soul. He only is able to save and to destroy. In view of this James asks: "By what superior holiness and wisdom do you judge your brother in Christ?" Let us draw nigh to God and stand for one moment in the presence of His holiness, and we will not be so quick to pass judgment upon others. In ourselves we are so short in wisdom and holiness that who are we that we should judge others? Rather should we be the last to judge them, but first to judge ourselves.

Before I conclude this message to you, I want to say in all fairness that there is a judgment that is right and Scriptural. Christians may be called upon to testify in a court of justice as well as in the church when it is imperative to deal with a sinning brother who continues in rebellion against the Word of God. However, the subject in James's Epistle is not civil government nor church discipline, but the sin of faultfinding, brother against brother.

If it falls our lot to pass judgment on anyone, let us be certain we are not uncharitable or inconsiderate to judge another's motives; rather, let it be done in love and with the fullest possible knowledge of the facts in question. But if we must question the motives or actions of another Christian, it is always more profitable to speak *to* him than *of* him.

Thy will, O Lord, not mine,
  Teach me to say;
Not my will, Lord, but Thine,
  I would obey;
Then shall I know the joy,
And Thy Name glorify,
When I, on earth, shall try
  To follow Thee.

My weakness, Lord, I own,
  From day to day;
I listen for Thy voice
  To lead the way;
Oh, wilt Thou send the light
To make my pathway bright,
And show me what is right,
  The only way.

I cannot see just where
  The Spirit leads,
But know that Christ is there,
  Who intercedes;
Oh, help me now to rest
On Jesus' loving breast,
Till He shall manifest
  His love in me!

SINNING THROUGH
SIDE-STEPPING GOD

James 4:13-17

13. Go to now, ye that say, To day or to morrow we will go into such a city, and continue there a year, and buy and sell, and get gain:

14. Whereas ye know not what shall be on the morrow. For what is your life? It is even a vapour, that appeareth for a little time, and then vanisheth away.

15. For that ye ought to say, If the Lord will, we shall live, and do this, or that.

16. But now ye rejoice in your boastings: all such rejoicing is evil.

17. Therefore to him that knoweth to do good, and doeth it not, to him it is sin.

In this closing paragraph of Chapter Four, the Apostle uses an expression that is, so far as I know, used nowhere else in the New Testament save Chapter Five, verse one: *"Go to now."* It is a verbal gesture used, I believe, to arouse interest and call attention to what is about to follow, like the gesture of a public speaker who is not maintaining the fullest interest of his audience. James has something further of importance to say, and he wants the closest attention of his readers.

A common sin is dealt with here. It is that of practical atheism, planning without taking God into account. Here are those who plan their lives as if their own wills were final and supreme. They say: "To day or to morrow we will go into such a city, and continue there a year, and buy and sell, and get gain" (4:13). This is bold human presumption giving no thought whatever to divine providence.

Just what is wrong with this kind of presumptuous planning? In the first place, it calculates on a time element in the future, a sphere into which no man can project with assurance. The cleverest human mind is unable to predict with accuracy what will take place tomorrow, knowing that his predictions must come to pass. It is quite possible that my plans and predictions may turn out tomorrow as I arranged them in my mind today, but of this I cannot be certain. In a moment we shall permit James to show us the weakness in such faulty reasoning, but now let us examine verse thirteen a bit more closely.

The persons here addressed are businessmen, merchants, employers, or employees, giving thought to careful planning in their business dealings; but, mind you, it is not the careful planning that James here condemns. He is not speaking against preparing for the future. Frankly, we can do with more careful planning and good business sense in our churches. If some businessmen operated their personal business in the way they try to run the business of the church, they would soon be bankrupt. Quite frequently the Lord brings to my mind the words, "Not slothful in business" (Rom. 12:11). As a pastor and leader of a local church I feel keenly the responsibility that is upon me. In all of our business dealings, we must remain above reproach and censure. We cannot afford to fail through unwise planning, or purchasing, or in assuming unjustifiable debt. I am not forgetting the absolute necessity for faith in Christian experience, but let us not place the blame for our failures on God nor charge it to lack of faith in God.

Look once again at verse thirteen and you will observe that God is not in these plans at all. James is concerned with those who seek plans for the future, without God. The men in our verse are engaged in a dangerous practice. They are looking at tomorrow, nay more, they are looking a year ahead, omitting God completely. Herein lay the sin.

None of us has any right to plan tomorrow, next week, next month, or next year without consulting God. The disposal of our tomorrows is not committed entirely to us. We cannot plan independently of God to go here or there, or how long our journey shall take, or how much money we shall have at the end of a given period of time. None of these things is in our hands. Here is a form of worldliness, I suppose, that has tainted most of us; but we may be certain that any plans we make for the future, with no thought of God, can offer only false hope and false confidence.

"Whereas, ye know not what shall be on the morrow. For what is your life? It is even a vapour, that appeareth for a little time, and then vanisheth away" (4:14). It is possible for this very reason that the Lord Jesus said: "Take therefore no thought for the morrow: for the morrow shall take thought for the things of itself. Sufficient unto the day is the evil thereof" (Matt. 6:34). How foolish to be anxious concerning the unknown! While none of us can know what the future holds, we can know the One who holds the future; therefore we do well if we heed the proverb which says: "Boast not thyself of to morrow; for thou knowest not what a day may bring forth" (Prov. 27:1).

Take into account the transitoriness of life: we have no lease on it, no guarantee that we will be among the living tomorrow. *"For what is your life? It is even a vapour, that appeareth for a little time, and then vanisheth away."* Our lives are like the morning mist, a wisp of cloud, a puff of smoke, that appear for a few moments, and then vanish. Our Lord spoke of the rich man who sought great riches in order that he might spend his years in ease, but in his plans left God out entirely. "But God said unto him, Thou fool, this night thy soul shall be required of thee: then whose shall those things be, which thou hast provided?" (Luke 12:20). Such a man may be a wise planner and a clever schemer in the eyes of the world, but God calls him a fool.

Beloved, we are dying men and women, and we do not know at what moment our earthly pilgrimage will cease. Tomorrow may dawn for us, or it may not. If it does, we know not what divine providence has in store, what change of circumstance, what turn of events.

This reminds me of my friend John Myers. We were together in Boca Raton, Florida, and discussed his plans to go to Japan as a missionary. Five weeks later I received word that John had drowned in the very swimming pool in which we stood together to talk about his future. But I rejoice that his plans included God.

"For that ye ought to say, If the Lord will, we shall live, and do this, or that" (4:15). The fact of life's uncertainty and our ignorance of what the future holds should move us to consider the will of God in all our ways. Before Paul left the brethren in Ephesus, he said: "I will return again unto you, *if God will*" (Acts 18:21). Writing to the Corinthians, he said: "But I will come to you shortly, if the Lord will . . ." (1 Cor. 4:19). The will of the Lord was on Paul's lips, and the words flowed from his pen because it was the desire of his heart.

The will of the Lord is always best for His children. Paul calls His will "good . . . acceptable . . . perfect" (Rom. 12:2). It is His will that we must consider in all our affairs, whether business, religious, national, civic, or domestic. Life for the Christian is not a game of chance, nor are its issues decided with the flip of a coin. All is in God's hands, and since He has a plan and a purpose for each of our lives, we cannot afford to make decisions independent of Him. I know that most people do not favor this language today. Few people prefer God's will; fewer still refer to God's will. But the true Christian has no other choice. I confess to you, I would not want this whole world in my grasp and be outside of God's will, for "the world passeth away, and the lust thereof: but he that doeth the will of God abideth for ever" (1 John 2:17).

It is both natural and good for us that we have desires in this life, but our desires should be only those things that God desires for us. David wrote: "Delight thyself also in the Lord; and He shall give thee the desires of thine heart" (Psalm 37:4). If our desires draw us toward the Lord, then we shall be satisfied, but if they lead us away from God because they are sinful, we must expect disappointment. The will of God is doubtless the secret to victory in Christian living and power in service.

"But now ye rejoice in your boastings: all such rejoicing is evil" (4:16). The Christians were not only guilty of leaving God out of their plans and of boasting what they were going to do, but they were glorying in their boastings. Oh, beloved, this is indeed most sinful. Honestly now, what do we have that we did not receive (1 Cor. 4:7)? If we only knew what the future had to offer us and that our planning without God cannot meet with success, we would consider Him in all things. After all, our plannings and boastings in the flesh are not a sign of confidence and security, but are an evidence of insecurity. The braggart is covering up an inward lack by his outward boast. William Henley's famous poem "Invictus" reveals this lack.

> "Out of the night that covers me,
>   Black as the Pit from pole to pole,
> I thank whatever gods may be
>   For my unconquerable soul.
>
> "In the fell clutch of circumstance
>   I have not winced nor cried aloud.
> Under the bludgeonings of chance
>   My head is bloody, but unbowed.
>
> "Beyond this place of wrath and tears
>   Looms but the Horror of the shade,
> And yet the menace of the years
>   Finds, and shall find, me unafraid.
>
> "It matters not how strait the gate,
>   How charged with punishments the scroll,
> I am the master of my fate;
>   I am the captain of my soul."

Such boasting is nothing more than whistling in the dark, trying to make his way through the graveyard of his own failure and fears. James says that all such boasting is evil.

The chapter concludes with one of the most significant and searching definitions of sin to be found anywhere in the Bible.

"Therefore to him that knoweth to do good, and doeth it not, to him it is sin" (4:17). Here sin is defined negatively. Not only is it sinful to do and say things that are wrong, but it is equally sinful to refuse to do what is right. Here is a form of sin we might ponder seriously. It is possible that some of you are guilty of committing sin as you sit in the worship service. You may not be chargeable for committing what God has forbidden, but you might be guilty of neglecting what He has commanded.

Let me apply the principle of verse seventeen to the main burden of our paragraph expounded in this chapter. James has been dealing with the Christian and God's will. He has been deploring the sin of side-stepping God's will while planning for the future. Now we know that such action is wrong; therefore if we continue to shut God out of our plans, we commit sin.

Responsibility accompanies knowledge. When we commit sin unwittingly, it is wrong; but when we commit sin willfully and knowingly, we are open for a more severe chastisement. Our knowledge of what is right makes us guilty of sin if we do not do it. Jesus said: "If ye know these things, happy are ye if ye do them" (John 13:17). We must not only cease to do evil, we must strive to do what we know is right. Some of you know you should support the prayer meeting, but you do not do it. Some of you know you should be giving more time to God's work, but you do not do it. Some of you know you should be giving more money to God, but still you withhold. Some of you know you should be giving yourself to His Word, but still you continue to neglect it. Some of you know you should visit the sick and shut-ins, but you will not bother. I can only quote our closing verse. "Therefore to him that knoweth to do good, and doeth it not, to him it is sin" (4:17). I fear many Christians will miss our Lord's commendation, "Well done, thou good and faithful servant: thou hast been faithful over a few things, I will make thee ruler over many things: enter thou into the joy of thy lord" (Matt. 25:21).

I am satisfied with Jesus,
  He has done so much for me,
He has suffered to redeem me,
  He has died to set me free.

He is with me in my trials,
  Best of friends of all is He;
I can always count on Jesus,
  Can He always count on me?

I can hear the voice of Jesus
  Calling out so pleadingly,
"Go and win the lost and straying";
  Is He satisfied with me?

When my work on earth is ended,
  And I cross the mystic sea,
Oh, that I could hear Him saying,
  "I am satisfied with thee."

I am satisfied, I am satisfied,
  I am satisfied with Jesus,
But the question comes to me.
  As I think of Calvary,
Is my Master satisfied with me?

CONDEMNATION THROUGH COVETOUSNESS

James 5:1-6

1. Go to now, ye rich men, weep and howl for your miseries that shall come upon you.

2. Your riches are corrupted, and your garments are moth-eaten.

3. Your gold and silver is cankered; and the rust of them shall be a witness against you, and shall eat your flesh as it were fire. Ye have heaped treaure together for the last days.

4. Behold, the hire of the labourers who have reaped down your fields, which is of you kept back by fraud, crieth: and the cries of them which have reaped are entered into the ears of the Lord of sabaoth.

5. Ye have lived in pleasure on the earth, and been wanton; ye have nourished your hearts, as in a day of slaughter.

6. Ye have condemned and killed the just; and he doth not resist you.

The Apostle launches out in a bold attack against that spirit of covetousness everywhere condemned in Scripture. Commentators are divided in their opinion as to exactly who it is that James has in mind. Are they the saved or the unsaved? Some able teachers are of the opinion that he turns, in this paragraph (verses 1-6), from the believer to the unbeliever. I am inclined to accept this position in the light of the context, and in the marked transition in verse seven—*"Be patient therefore, brethren . . ."*

This is the third time James refers to the rich. In 1:10 he commends the rich believer for having taken his place humbly as a needy sinner; in 2:1-7 he condemns the believer who gives preferential treatment to the rich who enter the church; but in our present study he condemns quite sharply the wicked rich. There is solemn teaching here for every Christian, seeing the miserable end of the godless, covetous rich, that he should never covet riches nor unwisely use that which he has come by honestly.

"Go to now, ye rich men, weep and howl for your miseries that shall come upon you" (5:1). We dare not assume from these opening words that James thinks it is wrong to have riches. Such a wrong assumption is cleared away in the verses that follow. The Bible speaks of some good and godly men who had riches, as Abraham, Job, Joseph of Arimathaea, and others. The Bible nowhere condemns wealth as such, if it is acquired honestly and distributed wisely; but well might any rich man weep and howl who comes by his wealth dishonestly and spends it selfishly, knowing the awful reckoning that awaits him. It rejoices my heart whenever I meet a Christian who has riches, and at the same time lives modestly while he distributes generously to the Lord's work. The Spirit of God uses the words "weep and howl" in other places in Scripture (Isa. 15:3; Joel 1:5), and they express the awful agony of those whose money was their god and who lived selfishly. The rich man in hell who cried: "I am tormented in this flame" (Luke 16:24) is a case in point.

While it is true that a future judgment awaits the ungodly, James might have been referring to the destruction of Jerusalem, predicted by our Lord (Matt. 24:1, 2), and fulfilled only a few years after the Apostle wrote his Epistle. Although the rich were killed and robbed of their possessions when Jerusalem was destroyed, the prophecy of James was not to have its complete fulfillment then. The miseries that were to come to pass were to extend to the "last days" (5:3), even "unto the coming of the Lord" (5:7). The covetous rich *of our own day* cannot possibly escape the condemnation described in James's message. Is he not pointing out some signs and sins of the last days preceding the return of our Lord Jesus Christ? Our day is marked by the struggle for pleasure and possessions. Getting gain and spending it selfishly to gratify the lusts of the flesh is as common a sin in our times as at any time in the history of man. Here the servant of God and of the Lord Jesus Christ fearlessly condemns a popular sin. Only a man in touch with God could display such courage.

"Your riches are corrupted, and your garments are motheaten. Your gold and silver is cankered; and the rust of them shall be a witness against you, and shall eat your flesh as it were fire. Ye have heaped treasure together for the last days" (5:2, 3). Lest any of you have been misled into believing that life consists in the abundance of things a man possesses, take heed! Here is plain talk. Possessions unused are really wasted. The corruption and spoiling are a witness against the owner. God does not hold a man chargeable because a certain sum of money, however large, passes through his hands; but he does make a man responsible for any amount that he withholds until it becomes cankered and corrupt.

If God were to hold back the necessities and good things of this life in proportion to that which His children and unbelievers withhold, we all would be dead in a short time. "The earth is the Lord's, and the fulness thereof" (Psa. 24:1), but He never hedges it about so that we never can have access to it. God never deposits His wealth so that we cannot reach it. He never hoards. The very possessions that men hoard away in their miserliness have corrupted from disuse, and that rust and corruption will one day rise up as a witness against them.

When God's day of reckoning comes the rust of unused possession will prick the sinner's conscience, but, alas, it will then be too late to do anything about it. Our Lord said: "Lay not up for yourselves treasures upon earth, where moth and rust doth corrupt, and where thieves break through and steal: But lay up for yourselves treasures in heaven, where neither moth nor rust doth corrupt, and where thieves do not break through nor steal" (Matt. 6:19, 20). Clothes and earthly things form a large part of the treasure laid up on earth, but when we live to get those things in abundance, we discover in the end that any amount of wealth, not used for a worthy purpose, becomes worthless. The "last days" are days of crisis during which we should be giving thought as to how much we can give to the work of the Lord and in helping others, not how much we can hold for ourselves. The latter is folly indeed. One blast from God and the sum total of our possessions would be gone. Oh, beloved, do you want to be separated from your possessions? Do you want to see them perish without any benefit? I trust not. God does not give us His precious metals to rust nor garments to be motheaten but as a means of assisting others in need.

No man can determine whether he is rich or poor by merely looking at his balance in the bank. He is not rich or poor according to what he *has* but according to what he *is*. Actually the rich men to whom James was writing were poor. They were covetous and avaricious, selfish and wanton, and no man in such a state is ever rich. He is a pauper.

Have you an unused treasure? It might be an unused Bible, an unused talent, unused time, unused money, or an unused life. An idle treasure is good for nothing. The writer has never had much of this world's goods to lose, but he imagines somewhat the awful feeling that must have gripped the hearts of many who suddenly lost all in the financial and economic collapse when the depression came. He had a few Christian friends who had been walking close to God and who found comfort and consolation in turning to Him in that dark hour; but many others who trusted in their riches were in utter despair, even to committing suicide. A dark and bitter end awaits every man "that layeth up treasure for himself, and is not rich toward God" (Luke 12:21). There is great folly in heaping together unused wealth for one's self, especially when the struggle to accumulate riches goes on under the very shadow of divine judgment. There is no safe place to store ill-gotten wealth.

"Behold, the hire of the labourers who have reaped down your fields, which is of you kept back by fraud, crieth: and the cries of them which have reaped are entered into the ears of the Lord of sabaoth" (5:4). This verse condemns one popular method of getting riches: namely, hiring men and driving them in order to squeeze out of them every possible penny. These men were rich to begin with, for they possessed "fields," that is, they were land-owners. They should have paid their employees a living wage, but instead, they forced them to labor for next to nothing. They were guilty of that which God's law condemned, namely, fraud. God had said: "Thou shalt not defraud thy neighbour, neither rob him: the wages of him that is hired shall not abide with thee all night until the morning" (Lev. 19:13). Instead of paying their hired help what they were worth, they held back a portion for themselves, thereby defrauding them.

Elsewhere God's law makes it doubly clear that such a procedure is wrong—"Thou shalt not oppress an hired servant that is poor and needy, whether he be of thy brethren, or of thy strangers that are in thy land within thy gates: At his day thou shalt give him his hire, neither shall the sun go down upon it; for he is poor, and setteth his heart upon it: lest he cry against thee unto the Lord, and it be sin unto thee." (Deut. 24:14, 15). Such grasping covetousness and avarice will be met by swift judgment from Almighty God, for He has said: "I will come near to you to judgment; and I will be a swift witness . . . against those that oppress the hireling in his wages" (Mal. 3:5). Without engaging myself in the long unsettled dispute between capital and labor, I will merely say that no labor leader ever spoke out more severely and sternly against the unfair practices of some employers who pay laborers less than a living wage in order that they might add more to their vast possessions. Let us remind ourselves that such a practice is labeled "fraud" by God, and it will cry out against the wicked rich in the day of judgment even as Abel's blood cried out against Cain (Gen. 4:10). Wealth may give a man a certain power in this life, but he might better be careful that he never abuses nor misuses that power. Beware of social injustice in your own heart!

"The cries of them which have reaped [or labored] are entered into the ears of the Lord of sabaoth." The rich may have been deaf to the cries of the oppressed, but God was not. They closed their ears to the appeals of the distressed, but God heard them. I am thinking at this point of the oppression which the taskmasters of Egypt brought to bear upon the children of Israel. "And the

Lord said, I have surely seen the affliction of my people which are in Egypt, and have heard their cry by reason of their taskmasters; for I know their sorrows" (Exodus 3:7).

Our God is the Lord of the hosts of heaven. No amount of economic or military power can withstand Him. It was in the name of the Lord of Sabaoth that David withstood Goliath (1 Sam. 17:45). God never stands by idly while the poor are being oppressed. Whatever else James has in mind, he certainly is not omitting the fact that God is on the side of those who are wronged. Human might can never overcome divine right. God regards every act of cruelty and oppression. Those who are guilty of such can shut it out of their ears, but it will be heard by God every time. Let every helpless victim of oppressors be comforted. God is not an uninterested bystander. He is deeply moved by what He sees, and "He forgetteth not the cry of the humble" (Psalm 9:12). The day of reckoning must come. We read: "Thou shalt neither vex a stranger, nor oppress him: for ye were strangers in the land of Egypt. Ye shall not afflict any widow, or fatherless child. If thou afflict them in any wise, and they cry at all unto me, I will surely hear their cry; And my wrath shall wax hot, and I will kill you with the sword; and your wives shall be widows, and your children fatherless" (Exodus 22:21-24). "Masters, give unto your servants that which is just and equal; knowing that ye also have a Master in heaven" (Col. 4:1).

James continues with a charge against the rich because of their lavish indulgence: "Ye have lived in pleasure on the earth, and been wanton; ye have nourished your hearts, as in a day of slaughter" (5:5). While some rich persons oppress the poor and hoard their ill-gotten gains, they spend freely enough upon themselves so as to gratify their own lustful desires. Look again at the contrast between the rich man and the beggar in Luke 16:19-21. Many rich people pamper their own likings while the poor around them suffer from lacking the bare necessities of life.

Stage and screen players are examples of extravagant spending of the rich. Show business, so called, has done much to corrupt our way of life. Luxury and gaiety are characteristic of America's wealthier class. They are "lovers of pleasures more than lovers of God" (2 Tim. 3:4). One movie actress gave a party on her luxurious estate, and after the guests arrived, it was reported that she had five thousand dollars' worth of imported champagne poured into the swimming pool. Swimming in the pool was part of the evening's activities. This is but one illustration of wantonness and wild gaiety among the rich, and it is mild compared with other stories we have heard and read about.

In a very true sense, however, the rich man's wealth is his undoing, for he fattens himself for the day of slaughter. The picture in these words, *"ye have nourished your hearts, as in a day of slaughter,"* is that of cattle or hogs who do nothing but feed themselves, unconscious that they are but fattening themselves for their own slaughter. So will it be with those who engaged in self-indulgence like greedy swine, realizing little the judgment that awaits them. Their doom is certain. The fatter the livestock, the more ready they are for the slaughter. Beware, oh reader!

In Noah's day the people were eating and drinking, marrying and giving in marriage, and they knew not how near divine judgment was until the flood came and swept them all away (Matt. 24:36-39). The men of Sodom and Gomorrah were living in sin, when suddenly the Lord rained fire and brimstone upon those cities (Gen. 19:23-25). Jesus said that as it was in the days of Noah and the flood, and Sodom and Gomorrah, "Even thus shall it be in the day when the Son of man is revealed" (Luke 17:26-30). It happened to Belshazzar. While he engaged in a drunken feast, out of the sleeve of the night the hand of God wrote his doom upon the palace wall, and he never saw the morning light (Dan. 5). Yes, when our Lord returns to judge the earth, men will die with God's judgment being meted out to them in the measure of their wicked living. Again I say, let all who engage in godless luxury take seriously these Biblical examples of a horrible end unless they repent.

And now, James has a final word to the wicked rich. "Ye have condemned and killed the just; and he doth not resist you" (5: 6). There are two possible interpretations of this verse, both of which are accepted by scholars of equal repute. Some say the Just One killed is our Lord Jesus Christ, who unresistingly was slain by wicked men, and that the poor who are being oppressed are to follow in His steps: that is, they are to bear in silence the wrong and shame heaped upon them by the wicked rich. In this connection we are reminded of Peter's words to the assembly in Solomon's Porch: "Ye denied the Holy One and the Just" (Acts 3:14), and also the words of Stephen before the Sanhedrin (Acts 7:52). Those who thus interpret verse six advocate that as Christ was led to His slaughter as a lamb dumb, and opened not his mouth, so believers should not complain of any wrong treatment inflicted upon them by unbelievers.

Other teachers hold that James has here in view some great men of God who were slain, such as the prophets (Matt. 23:37), Stephen (Acts 7:60), and others who died as martyrs, of whom James, according to tradition, is reported to be one. We are to expect a heartless indifference on the part of the world.

In summing up this message, let me remind you, and my own soul, of some of the perils of prosperity. Few of us can say with Paul: "I know how to abound" (Phil. 4:12). Sometimes we fail to acknowledge that honestly gained prosperity is a gift from God, no matter how hard one had to work in order to obtain it. No matter how much intelligence, influence, or ingenuity we might have and use with which to gain wealth, God must be recognized as the Giver of all. Then, too, whatever we possess in material wealth, it is all a trust from God. He gave it, and He can take it from us at will. We are but stewards. Someone has asked: "If tomorrow you were to lose all of your material possessions and your health, would you have anything left?"

On that bright and golden morning when the Son of Man shall
    come,
  And the radiance of His glory we shall see;
When from every clime and nation He shall call His people home—
  What a gath'ring of the ransomed that will be!

When the blest who sleep in Jesus at His bidding shall arise
  From the silence of the grave, and from the sea;
And with bodies all celestial they shall meet Him in the skies—
  What a gath'ring and rejoicing there will be!

When our eyes behold the City, with its "many mansions" bright,
  And its river, calm and restful, flowing free—
When the friends that death has parted shall in bliss again unite—
  What a gath'ring and a greeting there will be!

Oh, the King is surely coming, and the time is drawing nigh,
  When the blessed day of promise we shall see;
Then the changing "in a moment," "in the twinkling of an eye,"
  And for ever in His presence we shall be.

PATIENCE THROUGH
THE PAROUSIA

James 5:7-12

7. Be patient therefore, brethren, unto the coming of the Lord. Behold, the husbandman waiteth for the precious fruit of the earth, and hath long patience for it, until he receive the early and latter rain.

8. Be ye also patient; stablish your hearts; for the coming of the Lord draweth nigh.

9. Grudge not one against another, brethren, lest ye be condemned: behold, the judge standeth before the door.

10. Take, my brethren, the prophets, who have spoken in the name of the Lord, for an example of suffering affliction, and of patience.

11. Behold, we count them happy which endure. Ye have heard of the patience of Job, and have seen the end of the Lord; that the Lord is very pitiful, and of tender mercy.

12. But above all things, my brethren, swear not, neither by heaven, neither by the earth, neither by any other oath: but let your yea be yea; and your nay, nay; lest ye fall into condemnation.

This life is so marked by pressure and problems that the outlook in the present is not very bright for many of God's children. The social problem arising out of the conflict between capital and labor, employer and employee, of which the Apostle has just written, is but a sample of the causes of hardship the Christian must face. Should believers seek a cure for the world's social ills apart from Jesus Christ? Personally, I desire that the part of the world that touches my life shall be influenced for good, and I trust that I am exercising myself to that end; but frankly, I can see no cure-all for the mounting multiplicity of problems before the personal return of Jesus Christ.

In view of the certainty of Christ's return, James exhorts us to patience. "Be patient therefore, brethren, unto the coming of the Lord . . ." (5:7). It is quite clear that the believers in the early church looked forward to Christ's return at which time He will set things right. The outlook for Paul presented no bright cloud on the horizon, but the prospect in the uplook was most encouraging, "Looking for that blessed hope, and the glorious appearing of the great God and our Saviour Jesus Christ" (Titus 2:13). These Christians were "waiting for the coming of our Lord Jesus Christ" (1 Cor. 1:7). They were looking for His coming (Phil. 3:20). Likewise were the saints at Colosse (Col. 3:4), and Thessalonica (1 Thess. 1:9, 10). These are but a few references on this vital subject of Christ's return that is taught throughout the entire Scriptures.

The hope of our Lord's coming again was not fulfilled as those in the early church expected it, but even for them it was not cherished in vain. It is both a comforting hope (1 Thess. 4:18) and a purifying hope (1 John 3:2, 3). Knowing that He must come to take over the reins of government and put right every wrong in this sin-scarred world, James exhorts us to patient endurance. Our Apostle was sharing a blessed truth with every other divinely inspired writer of the New Testament when he assured them that the Lord will come again. In view of His return we can afford to be patient. We need never pursue revenge nor precipitate a lawsuit nor persist in claiming our rights. No, we need only practice patience. "Let your moderation be known unto all men. The Lord is at hand" (Phil. 4:5). His appearing will put down the cruel oppressors of His church and the persecutors of His followers. If we are called to suffering and reproach, let us bear it with patience. The presence of Him who will bring His rewards for His own will likewise bring retribution to His enemies.

Few things, if any, in the life of a believer, are more difficult to practice than patience in the midst of trial or persecution. Yet, patience until He comes is exactly what we are exhorted to practice. Moreover, it is the one thing of which most stand in need.

The Scriptures remind us, "Ye have need of patience" (Heb. 10:
36). You see, according to our scheme of reckoning, God moves
very slowly. No sooner had our first parents sinned when God
gave the promise of the Redeemer; but the world waited approx-
imately forty centuries for His first coming. "But when the fulness
of the time was come, God sent forth his Son, made of a woman,
made under the law" (Gal. 4:4). We wait for the fulfillment of
the promise of His second coming, and we need patience as we
wait, for "be not ignorant of this one thing, that one day is with
the Lord as a thousand years, and a thousand years as one day"
(2 Peter 3:8) . . . "The day of the Lord will come . . ." (2
Peter 3:10). When our Lord was here upon earth He promised
He would return (John 14:3). The first message He sent back
to earth after He ascended was the fact of His coming again
(Acts 1:11). His final word to the sons of men is: "Surely I come
quickly" (Rev. 22:20). "Be patient therefore, brethren, unto
the coming of the Lord."

An illustration of patient waiting is that of the farmer. "Behold, the husbandman waiteth for the precious fruit of the earth,
and hath long patience for it, until he receive the early and
latter rain." The farmer plants his grain, and then waits with
patience for the early rain in the fall, and the latter rain in the
spring, before he can gather the ripened harvest. The waiting
period for the farmer is never without its trials and testing. The
weather may be too hot, too cold, too dry, or too wet. Then,
too, there are the insect pests to contend with. Recently we spent
a holiday on a large farm owned and operated by a dear Christian
friend. The farmer and his sons worked long hours and very hard.
Every day found them active from twelve to fourteen hours, all
the while waiting patiently for the harvest.

We who are Christ's have many things to try our patience, but
we must endure with longsuffering. As we engage in holy service
and live holy lives, we may be certain that "in due season we shall
reap, if we faint not" (Gal. 6:9). Do not faint under tribulation,
for by it God is producing *patience* (Rom. 5:3). We are exhorted

not only to be sound in faith, but sound in *patience* as well (Titus 2:2). "Add to your faith . . . patience" (2 Peter 1:5, 6). It is not sufficient that we believe on the Lord Jesus Christ; we must "run with *patience* the race that is set before us . . . Looking unto Jesus . . ." (Heb. 12:1, 2). The certainty of His return is a challenge to purity, humble service, and watchful expectancy in spite of the trials. No farmer would want the sun to shine all of the time. If he did not have the clouds that bring the rain, his fields would turn into a desert. Every field must endure the change of climate which brings its storms of varied degrees. We are "God's husbandry" (1 Cor. 3:9): that is, we are God's tilled field, and we must with patience wait, and, if necessary, suffer, that our fruit may be brought forth in due season (Psalm 1:3). There is a day of harvest coming, the fruit of which is dependent upon our purity and patience.

The exhortation to longsuffering is not an appeal to stoical indifference to our trials and temptations. Our trouble is real, but however many the days and years be during which we must suffer, we can be certain that while "weeping may endure for a night, . . . joy cometh in the morning" (Psalm 30:5), the morning of His appearing. "When Christ, who is our life, shall appear, then shall ye also appear with Him in glory" (Col. 3:4), the glory that must follow the sufferings (1 Peter 5:1). It is plain from all of the foregoing that God would have His children face their trials realistically, but in patient expectation of our Lord's return. Eager as we might be for that day, we must wait quietly for the harvest. It is childish to sow seed in our little flower bed, and then to dig it up impatiently the day following because it did not yield the flower.

"Be ye also patient; stablish your hearts: for the coming of the Lord draweth nigh" (5:8). The word *"stablish"* might better be rendered *"strengthen."* The hope of our Lord's coming should strengthen our hearts. The Christians in the early church, at least the Apostles, did not give up when they failed to see Him come in their day. Abraham did not live to see the promised Seed of the woman, still "he staggered not at the promise of God through unbelief; but was strong in faith, giving glory to God" (Rom. 4:20). "He that shall come will come, and will not tarry" (Heb. 10:37). Let the very thought of it stablish, steady, strengthen you to meet, in triumph, the sorest trials of your life.

Our paragraph continues by teaching us not to become impatient with each other. "Grudge not one against another, brethren, lest ye be condemned: behold, the judge standeth before the door" (5:9). Grudging means grumbling and judging. When trials come to us we find it easy to murmur and complain in a censorious spirit. We must leave all judgment until the Judge comes, who, at His appearing, will judge the living and the dead. Vengeance will be meted out by Him at that day. If we take into our own hands the matter of judging, we ourselves will be judged for so doing (Matt. 7:1). Stop complaining one against another. Jesus alone is qualified to judge in all matters, and He stands at the door. Beware lest your trials wind you up and you wind up quarrelling with your brethren in Christ. Most likely those about whom you complain are not responsible for your troubles. Why not yield to the indwelling Holy Spirit, and your complaining will cease! With our Lord's return so near, we cannot afford to fall out with one another. We do well to ponder Abraham's philosophy when he said to Lot: "Let there be no strife, I pray thee, between me and thee . . . for we be brethren" (Gen. 13:8).

Having used the farmer as an illustration of patience, James now turns to the prophets. "Take, my brethren, the prophets, who have spoken in the name of the Lord, for an example of suffering affliction, and of patience" (5:10). Why should he choose the prophets to illustrate patience in suffering? The prophets were God's fearless spokesmen who condemned the sin of the people. Both Jeremiah and Daniel are examples of suffering prophets. Jesus said: "O Jerusalem, Jerusalem, thou that killest the prophets, and stonest them which are sent unto thee, how often would I have gathered thy children together, even as a hen gathereth her chickens under her wings, and ye would not" (Matt.

23:37)! Stephen asked of the Sanhedrin: "Which of the prophets have not your fathers persecuted?" (Acts 7:52). Yet they
were examples of suffering affliction and of patience in spite of
the fact that the persecution was sometimes at the instigation of
their own people (1 Thess. 2:14, 15). If these exemplary men
suffered uncomplainingly, we should follow their example. We
count them *"happy"* (or *blessed*), says James, so why then should
we shrink from the same experience? Indeed all suffering saints
are counted blessed, not merely by men, but by Him who bore
the severest contradiction of sinners (Matt. 5:10).

In his last illustration of patience in severe trial, James refers
to Job. "Ye have heard of the patience of Job, and have seen the
end of the Lord; that the Lord is very pitiful, and of tender
mercy" (5:11). Few men, apart from our Lord Jesus Christ, were
made to be the innocent sufferer like Job. He lost his servants,
livestock, property, and finally his sons in death. Then Job himself was smitten with sore boils from the soles of his feet to the
crown of his head. The end of Job's story, however, reads thus:
"So the Lord blessed the latter end of Job more than his beginning" (Job 42:12).

And what does this all prove? "That the Lord is very pitiful,
and of tender mercy." The trouble that comes to God's children
is not without purpose. Joseph, too, suffered at the hands of his
brethren, but in the end he could say: "But as for you, ye thought
evil against me; but God meant it unto good . . ." (Gen. 50:20).

The life story of every man who lives in the will of God, regardless of how much trouble he passes through, must end thus,
for "we know that all things work together for good to them that
love God, to them who are the called according to His purpose"
(Rom. 8:28). Our trials are not meaningless. Give God time, and
His purposes will be made clear in "the end." Frankly, as I read
the Book of Job, I am not overly impressed at times with the
patience of Job, but I am deeply moved with "the end of the
Lord." Be patient, brethren. God is near to every soul that is
being tried and tested, and His nearness will be even more prec-

ious at the coming of His Son. In that day we will be face to face with Him who does all things well.

Before we conclude our study of this paragraph, I ask you to share with me some thoughts on verse twelve. "But above all things, my brethren, swear not, neither by heaven, neither by the earth, neither by any other oath: but let your yea be yea; and your nay, nay; lest ye fall into condemnation" (5:12). I have felt that too little space is given in the commentaries to a discussion of this verse. Some expositors have made no comment whatever. While it is true that this one verse is given over to a subject that seems almost to stand alone in James's Epistle, there are numerous other Scriptures which throw light upon the general topic of oaths.

After having given considerable thought to this verse, I would say that we have before us a big subject, namely, *The Sacredness of Speech*. When one considers James's source of thought and material, one dares not to pass lightly over this verse. As with other statements in his Epistle, James depended upon the teaching of our Lord Jesus Christ. Before we discuss the general topic of oaths, let us read together some words of our Lord. "Again, ye have heard that it hath been said by them of old time, Thou shalt not forswear thyself, but shalt perform unto the Lord thine oaths: But I say unto you, Swear not at all; neither by heaven; for it is God's throne: Nor by the earth; for it is His footstool: neither by Jerusalem; for it is the city of the great King. Neither shalt thou swear by thy head, because thou canst not make one hair white or black. But let your communication be, Yea, yea; Nay, nay: for whatsoever is more than these cometh of evil" (Matt. 5:33-37).

Among various forms of the oath, there is that of *profanity*. Here is doubtless one of the most senseless and disgusting of sins. Men and women are known to call upon the holy name of God and of His Son Jesus Christ to express feelings of anger, disapproval, and overemphasis. This practice seems to me to be well nigh inhuman. If wild beasts could speak, I can visualize such a practice among them, but among civilized people, never. Yet there are few places in the world where one can go and not hear this cheap, common expression of a wicked heart; and never let it be said that profanity does not emanate from an evil heart, for our Lord said: "O generation of vipers, how can ye, being evil, speak good things? for out of the abundance of the heart the mouth speaketh. A good man out of the good treasure of the heart bringeth forth good things: and an evil man out of the evil treasure bringeth forth evil things. But I say unto you, That every idle word that men shall speak, they shall give account thereof in the day of judgment. For by thy words thou shalt be justified, and by thy words thou shalt be condemned" (Matt. 12:34-37). I doubt that there is anything that men pay less attention to than their words, as though it matters little what they say. But it does matter. What we say will be weighed as carefully in the day of judgment as what we do. Our words show the condition of our hearts. "Death and life are in the power of the tongue . . ." (Prov. 18:21). "Every man's heart is a storehouse, and his words show what he keeps there. What is said on the spur of the moment is sometimes better evidence of a man's disposition than what he says deliberately, for the latter may be calculated hypocrisy" (Alfred Plummer).

The Third Commandment says: "Thou shalt not take the name of the Lord thy God in vain; for the Lord will not hold him guiltless that taketh His name in vain" (Exod. 20:7). When we compare this Commandment with the Ninth, which says: "Thou shalt not bear false witness against thy neighbour" (Exod. 20:16), we see that God is, in these two commandments, protecting both His Name and our name. He demands that His creatures be concerned with the honor of His Name. His Name in Scripture is always a revelation of His nature. God is holy, just, all-wise, all-powerful, His many attributes and characteristics being revealed in His Names. Whenever an ancient scribe copied the sacred manuscripts, he would stop before writing the Name of God, bathe himself all over, then return to his writing table with a new, hitherto-unused pen, and then proceed to write the Name of God in whatever form it appeared. It was always in holy awe and reverence that a scribe even read any of the Names of God.

The Third Commandment enjoins a solemn responsibility upon all men everywhere. We may not, at any time, or under any circumstances, use God's Holy Name loosely or frivolously; and yet, many persons in all walks of life are so spiritually and morally impoverished that they have to fill in their vocabulary with trite and trivial language involving the Names of God and of Christ. Even among Christians there are various subterfuges devised such as "gee" and "golly." It has been suggested that these are but substitutes for "Jesus" and "God." Do not imagine that you are guiltless just because you do not openly take in vain the Names of God and His Son Jesus Christ.

Neither is it necessary to mention God's Name in order to profane it. Our Lord covered this point when He said: "Swear not . . . neither by heaven . . . nor by the earth." There were, and still are, those Orientals, Jews among them, who swear by heaven or earth. Even in our day it is not uncommon to hear such expressions as "good heavens," "for heaven's sake," "heaven help you," or "by the stars of heaven." But no man can call upon God's creative work in an oath and omit God Himself, for by thus speaking they call upon the Creator. We cannot disassociate the Creator from His creation. He is the Owner of all things, Heaven being His throne and earth His footstool. Every oath is a reference to a deity. It is high time that someone spoke out in solemn tones against the cheap, common cursing and swearing so prevalent today. Such an oath will bring one "into condemnation."

The oath takes on another form of swearing, not in the same category as profane cursing. I am thinking now of what is generally known as the legal oath. The words of our Lord, "Swear not at all," are interpreted by some groups, such as The Society of Friends and Quakers, to be absolute and not relative, thereby ruling out even the legal oath as required in a court of law. If we accept this view, then we must conclude that there are no lawful oaths. But is such a view tenable? The present writer thinks not. When Scripture is compared with Scripture, it is clear that throughout the entire Bible there are passages where the oath is commanded by God. Certainly a point to be made here is that men cannot escape the responsibility of an oath even though they omit the Name of God. "If a man vow a vow unto the Lord, or swear an oath to bind his soul with a bond; he shall not break his word, he shall do according to all that proceedeth out of his mouth" (Num. 30:2).

Think with me a bit on a significant verse in Hebrews. "For when God made promise to Abraham, because He could swear by no greater, He sware by Himself" (Heb. 6:13). Here it is stated that God, when He made a promise to Abraham (Gen. 22:16, 17), confirmed it with an oath. The promise and the oath were given by God at the same time. An *oath* is a solemn confirmation, or attestation, of a statement which appeals to a higher authority. Now since there can be no higher power than God, "He sware by Himself." Later Zacharias referred to the oath which God made to Abraham (Luke 1:73), and Stephen, in his testimony before the Jewish authorities, did likewise (Acts 7:17). Peter, on the day of Pentecost, makes mention of an oath with which God had sworn to David (Acts 2:30, 31). See Psalm 132:11. There being no one higher than Himself to whom to appeal in confirmation of His intention, He appealed to His own eternal and perfect Being. He is *omniscient,* hence He cannot make a promise the future of which is unknown to Him, nor can He forget what He has promised. He is *omnipotent,* so that there is no power in all the universe that can prevent Him from carrying out His promise, so there can be no question about the certainty of God performing what He has promised and sworn to. Actually God needed not to swear at all, since His promise is His Word and that cannot fail.

But why did God make the oath? It is customary for a man to swear, since an oath is more binding than his word. Abraham prevailed upon Eliezer to swear by an oath (Gen. 24:3). Joshua swore by an oath to confirm the league he made with the Gibeonites (Josh. 9:19). With the passing of time, the oath became common among frail men whose word could not be depended upon. Now God was willing to make an oath, not because He needed to, but because He knew how man depended upon it. It was another display of His condescending grace. He was actually staking His very existence on His Word.

Another interesting passage reads: "Thou shalt fear the Lord thy God, and serve Him, and shalt swear by His name" (Deut. 6:13). There is no contradiction between this verse and the third commandment in Exodus 20:7. The Third Commandment does not forbid taking an oath by God's Name, but it does forbid taking that Name in vain. The Israelites were permitted to take an oath by the Name of the Lord, but once they did so they must not in any way fail to keep their promise. To swear and then fail of the promise is to take His Name in vain. The oath was permitted by God, then, to place restraint upon fallen man's weakness and proneness to deceive and lie. One can see how easy it became to utter an oath lightly and indiscreetly in order to gain one's own ends. Such use of an oath is both dishonest and demoralizing.

There can be nothing in the essential nature of an oath which makes it wrong. Christ Himself answered with an oath when He responded to Caiaphas (Matt. 26:63, 64). Paul the Apostle confirmed his testimony on several occasions by calling upon God for a witness (2 Cor. 1:23; Gal. 1:20; Phil. 1:8). Even an angel was commissioned to "sware by Him that liveth for ever and ever" (Rev. 10:6). Boaz confirmed his promise of marriage to Ruth by an oath (Ruth 3:13). Swearing absolutely, then, is not condemned by either Jesus or James, but deceitful and needless swearing is.

An example of the wrong kind of an oath, which is sinful swearing, is the lodge oath taken by millions of men and women. I quote but one of many:

"Binding myself under no less a penalty than that of having my throat cut across, my tongue torn out by its roots, and buried in the rough sands of the sea at low-water mark, where the tide ebbs and flows twice in twenty-four hours, should I ever knowingly or willingly violate this my solemn oath and obligation as an Entered Apprentice Mason. So help me God, and keep me steadfast in the due performance of the same."

"Binding myself under no less a penalty than that of having my left breast torn open, my heart plucked out, and given as a prey to the wild beasts of the field and the fowls of the air . . ."

"Binding myself under no less a penalty than that of having my body severed in twain, my bowels taken from thence and burned to ashes, the ashes scattered to the four winds of heaven, so that no more trace or remembrance may be had of so vile and perjured a wretch as I, should I ever knowingly or willingly violate this my solemn obligation as a Master Mason. So help me God, and keep me steadfast in the due performance of the same."

Study carefully the above oath, and then ask yourself how any Christian in his right mind could possibly bind himself to such a penalty. Actually he has sworn to suicide, to "that of having my throat cut across." Such an unholy and profane oath dishonors God and His Holy Word, and ought never to be taken by any one, much less a Christian. Actually, the oath taken by the Entered Apprentice is not known by him until he hears it for the first time to swear to it. He has no choice but to swear allegiance to a blind oath. How utterly ridiculous! How foolish and absurd! My own conviction is that a Christian should never be a member of a lodge where he is unequally yoked with unbelievers and where he must swear to secrecy an oath he has never before heard.*

* Read *Lodges Examined by the Bible,* by John R. Rice, D.D.

Praise the Saviour, ye who know Him;
Who can tell how much we owe Him?
Gladly let us render to Him
   All we are and have.

"Jesus" is the name that charms us;
He for conflicts fits and arms us;
Nothing moves and nothing harms us,
   When we trust in Him.

Trust in Him, ye saints, for ever,
He is faithful, changing never;
Neither force nor guile can sever
   Those He loves from Him.

Keep us, Lord, oh, keep us cleaving
To Thyself, and still believing,
Till the hour of our receiving
   Promised joys in heaven.

Then we shall be where we would be,
Then we shall be what we should be;
Things which are not now, nor could be,
   Then shall be our own.

HELP AND HEALING
THROUGH PRAYER
AND PRAISE

James 5:13-18

13. Is any among you afflicted? let him pray. Is any merry? let him sing psalms.

14. Is any sick among you? let him call for the elders of the church; and let them pray over him, anointing him with oil in the name of the Lord:

15. And the prayer of faith shall save the sick, and the Lord shall raise him up; and if he have committed sins, they shall be forgiven him.

16. Confess your faults one to another, and pray one for another, that ye may be healed. The effectual fervent prayer of a righteous man availeth much.

17. Elias was a man subject to like passions as we are, and he prayed earnestly that it might not rain: and it rained not on the earth by the space of three years and six months.

18. And he prayed again, and the heaven gave rain, and the earth brought forth her fruit.

Ever since we commenced this series of devotional studies in the Epistle of James, I have been looking forward to these verses dealing with bodily healing. While I find no special delight in preaching from controversial passages in Holy Scripture, this portion of God's Word now before us has always intrigued me. I approach it prayerfully and carefully, seeking only the mind of the Holy Spirit. Please do not look for an exhaustive explanation in this treatise. Others before me have tried and come short. The wide disagreement and varied ideas of many commentators suggest that there is hidden truth here, some of which might never be clearly understood until we get to heaven.

Our present paragraph begins with the words: "Is any among

you afflicted? let him pray. Is any merry? let him sing psalms" (5:13). The *affliction* in this verse is certainly not confined to bodily illness, but rather does it mean "adversity," "suffering hardship." It is the affliction of stressing and strenuous circumstances often the lot of God's own people. How do we act when some hardship strikes? What is the first thing we do or say when trouble comes? There can be no satisfying relief in an angry outburst or in the utterance of an oath such as is forbidden in verse twelve. During my many years as a pastor, varied have been the reactions of different people to their hardships. Some have gone to pieces physically, demanding immediate medical attention. Others grumbled and complained like the children of Israel in the wilderness (Num. 11:1; 21:5, 6). A few have even bitterly blamed God for being unloving and unfair.

Just what should a child of God do when in the depths of adversity and affliction? *"Let him pray,"* says God's Word. Do not complain! Do not grumble! Pray! Every affliction is a call to prayer. There were times when I felt that God sent adversity to draw me closer to Him in prayer. This has been particularly true when I had become lax in my prayer life. We all must admit that affliction has a way of making the heart humble, contrite, and more dependent upon God.

To Manasseh, one of Israel's wicked kings, God spoke repeatedly but in vain. When the Lord sent the Assyrians, Manasseh was bound with fetters and taken captive to Babylon. "And when he was in affliction, he besought the Lord his God, and humbled himself greatly before the God of his fathers" (2 Chron. 33:11, 12). Oh, my brethren, when affliction comes, flee to God in prayer, for to this end He sends adversity to His own. The case of Manasseh is not an isolated one, but an illustration of one of God's methods of dealing with His own. His experience is recorded for our example.

When Sennacherib sent his blasphemous letter to Hezekiah, Judah's king, having read it, went straight up into the house of the Lord "and spread it before the Lord" (2 Kings 19:14). And before another sun had risen, the angel of God had smitten 185,-000 Assyrians. Here is an illustration of a man of God fleeing to God in prayer in the face of impending affliction. He did not wait until real trouble had backed him into a corner, but he sought God's help at once.

Have you ever weighed the possibility of God's sending adversity to prevent your going in the wrong direction? Jonah is a case in point. God had commissioned Jonah to go to Nineveh to preach, but Jonah, fleeing to Tarshish, hoped to escape from the presence of the Lord. Soon, however, he found himself in the whale's belly, the bowels of hell. Out of the depths of despair, in his affliction he cried to the Lord. The narrative reads: "When my soul fainted within me I remembered the Lord: and my prayer came in unto Thee, into Thine holy temple. They that observe lying vanities forsake their own mercy. But I will sacrifice unto Thee with the voice of thanksgiving; I will pay that that I have vowed. Salvation is of the Lord" (Jonah 2:7-9). God, forgiving His erring child, gave him another opportunity to serve Him in Nineveh. Here is a case of a man's flight from God and God's discipline by affliction to deter the wanderer. Had Jonah failed to repent, he might not have survived to experience the forgiveness of the Lord and the restoration to a life of usefulness. If you are a straying Christian reading these words, turn to God at once in your affliction. If the affliction has not come as yet, your turning may mean deliverance from it.

Sometimes the one suffering hardship is the most prone to neglect, and even to forget, prayer. The bent of the natural mind is to try everything else and turn to everyone else, before turning to God in prayer; but that one must come to the Lord in sincerity and humility only to find a ready and loving heart waiting to receive him. A child of God, however deep the distress, can show that he is a Christian by prayer.

Few children of God suffer more distress and hardship than David. Though hated and hunted by his enemies and sinning as grossly as any other man, he had learned the only way out of his distress was to *pray*. He wrote several of his prayers while in affliction. Here is one of them: "Hear my cry, O God; attend unto my prayer. From the end of the earth will I cry unto Thee, when my heart is overwhelmed: lead me to the rock that is higher than I" (Psalm 61:1, 2). David was doing what God wants all of His children to do: namely, "And call upon Me in the day of trouble: I will deliver thee, and thou shalt glorify Me" (Psalm 50:15).

Possibly some of you are wondering a bit just what to pray for. Although your first desire is to have the trial or affliction removed. be careful of such a prayer. As in the case of Paul, it may not be God's will to remove the affliction but rather to teach the afflicted one the sufficiency of His grace (2 Cor. 12:7-10). If you ask God to take away the affliction, be certain that you include in your prayer, even as did our Lord Jesus Christ in Gethsemane: "O my Father, if it be possible, let this cup pass from Me; nevertheless not as I will, but as Thou wilt" (Matt. 26:39).

By all means, pray for heavenly wisdom to act and speak wisely at such a time. (This we have dealt with in our comments on James 1:5.) There is no more difficult time to act wisely than when trials and affliction come to us. Although many foolish decisions are made and many foolish words spoken under the stress of tribulation, God promises wisdom to do and say the right thing.

Besides asking for wisdom when in trouble, we must take ample time to read quietly and meditatively from the Word of God. There is no wisdom compared with that which God has written in the Holy Scriptures and no true wisdom apart from it. The Psalmist wrote: "Thou through Thy commandments hast made me wiser than mine enemies" (Psalm 119:98). Let us be certain that we pray for divine wisdom, and pursue it in the Bible at all times, especially when affliction comes to us.

Another thing for which we should pray when in trouble is the needed grace and strength to bear up under the burden. This is most important for at least two reasons. First, hardship has a strange way of producing ill effects both mentally and physically upon the afflicted one. Secondly, the way we act in the time of trial and trouble may influence others to receive or reject Jesus Christ insofar as our ministry to them is concerned. Think it not strange if, at the Judgment Seat of Christ, you should be deprived of a reward for failing to bear a good testimony to God's sustaining grace while here upon earth. "What a Friend . . . !" "Oh, what a Peace!" "Tell it to Jesus!"

Returning now to our text in James we are faced with the other extreme of human emotions: namely, great delight or merriment of heart. In the first we are down in the depth of despair and distress; here we are on the heights of rejoicing—*"afflicted . . . merry."*

"Is any merry? let him sing psalms." How are we to give way to our extreme excitement? Notice, please, that the Christian's emotional experiences are very closely associated with his heavenly Father; inseparably so. In affliction, he is to pray; when all is well, let him sing. Prayer and praise, then, are two divinely given prescriptions to meet the needs of the child of God either in distress or in delight.

The merriment here is not the worldly, frolicsome gaiety so prevalent among unbelievers, but rather that wholesome cheerfulness of which the Bible speaks frequently. No one is edified when Christians engage in boisterous hilarity, but the believer who is cheerful in the Lord invariably brings blessing to others. He who is of good cheer is exhorted to *"sing praise."*(A.S.V.) When one is free from trouble, his state of mind is one of agreeableness and happiness, and such a condition is conducive to praise. When free from anxiety and affliction, the note of praise should be manifestly present.

Johnstone believes that the exact force of the original term will not permit the limited use of the word *"psalms"* so as to confine it to the Book of Psalms, however much that rich treasure Book delights the soul. It is more fully expressed in the words of Paul as, "Speaking to [or among] yourselves in psalms and hymns and spiritual songs, singing and making melody in your heart to the

Lord" (Eph. 5:19). When prosperity comes to us in any form, let us not lapse into a vain, self-confident, forgetful state of mind, but let us offer to our heavenly Father the sacrifice of praise (Heb. 13:15).

Here the word "continually" suggests the need for being joyful at all times, even when in affliction, for praise is an integral part of one's prayer life. "Be careful for nothing; but in every thing by prayer and supplication *with thanksgiving* let your requests be made known unto God" (Phil. 4:6). The spirit of thanksgiving, which is the spirit of praise, never should be absent from the Christian's life. A child of God can sing praise to God under the most strenuous and trying circumstances. When in prison, Paul and Silas "prayed and sang praises unto God: and the prisoners heard them" (Acts 16:25). This in turn led to the conversion of the jailkeeper and his family. Even though the voice be far from pleasant and melodious to the ears of others, we can make melody in our hearts to the Lord and radiate that joy to others. Praise is the highest expression of our prayers. Prayer and praise, then, are the Christian's normal outlet of his feelings.

In passing, permit me to testify to the personal benefit derived from the individual and congregational use of music, when coming from hearts in harmony with God. Its dignity and usefulness seem to be less appreciated with the passing of time. To remember God in our gladness by singing His praises is to the writer a mighty spiritual uplift. No doubt some of us have failed in not putting songs of praise into the minds and lips of our children along with teaching them the Scriptures and prayer. Let us keep far away from the empty, frivolous, suggestive songs of this world but concentrate on songs of praise to God which express the heart of one who finds joy and satisfaction in Him. The more a Christian knows of the purposes of God and yields to them, the more he will delight in singing His praises. The right kind of singing is often a favorable sign of the spiritual condition of God's people. And I am not speaking favorably of the chants of paid singers who know not the Lord, nor of the formalistic singing in public worship from unregenerated hearts. It is possible to get musical harmony and melody from uncoverted lives, but "The dead praise not the Lord" (Psalm 115:17). A Christian is one who has been redeemed by the precious blood of the Lord Jesus Christ, made alive in Him, and none but the living shall praise Him (Isa. 38:18). (See also Rev. 5:8, 9.) Beware, lest you lose your song!

> "In every joy that crowns my days,
>   In every pain I bear,
> My heart shall find delight in praise,
>   Or seek relief in prayer."

We come now to that much disputed passage on Divine Healing. I doubt if any of the works of God have as clever a satanic counterfeit as bodily healing. Moreover, no miracle that God ever performed among men is exalted above God's other mighty works as is healing. I sincerely believe in divine healing but not in divine healers.

Those who claim power to heal people as our Lord did are not as divine as they would have us believe. Their method of procedure is anything but divine. Modern "healers" claim to be doing Christ's work and the "greater works" of which He spoke (John 14:12); but why do modern "healers" go to all people when Christ said explicitly that His followers were to "go rather to the lost sheep of the house of Israel" (Matt. 10:6)? Why do modern healers appeal for money in their healing campaign when our Lord stated clearly that they were to take none (Luke 10:4)? Our Lord, as well as the Apostles also, not only healed the sick but raised the dead as well. I never have heard of any "healers" who have raised the dead. Attempting to duplicate the miracles of Jesus Christ is definitely not what James is writing about, for our Lord's miracles of healing, contrary to present day healings, were instantaneous, not gradual (Mark 1:42); complete, not partial (Matt. 8:15); permanent, not temporary (Luke 7:15).

Since present day "healers" are unable to duplicate Christ's miracles of healing and raising the dead, I am convinced that the types of healing performed by Him and His apostles are not for the day in which we live, nor have they ever been for the Church since the Bible was completed. However, there is a divine healing for this age, and I believe it to be that of which the Apostle James is speaking.

"Is any sick among you? let him call for the elders of the church; and let them pray over him, anointing him with oil in the name of the Lord: And the prayer of faith shall save the sick, and the Lord shall raise him up; and if he have committed sins, they shall be forgiven him" (5:14, 15). It is only right to point out that the "you" in this verse has a primary interpretation "to the twelve tribes which are scattered abroad" (1:1). This cannot be denied. Those to whom James addressed his message were most certainly "afflicted," and James precludes the possibility that some might be "sick"; but if we carry the application of the teaching in these verses to all believers during the Church Age, which is what we have been doing throughout these devotional studies, we must exercise great care so as not to depart from the meaning of the text.

The *first* thing to be noted is that the sick person, or persons, must call for the elders of the church. In all of the healing meetings that I have observed there has always been a great deal of effort put forth to bring the sick people to the public meeting. This is a violation of the Word of God and of good common sense. Only those well enough to attend the public gathering receive the benefits of the "healer's" work, while those who are too sick to go or be taken miss those benefits. Those confined to houses and institutions may not be worthy of the attention of present day "healers," but they are worthy of the attention of the Divine Healer. God told those who are sick to send for the elders of the church, not the preacher or evangelist.

As a pastor I feel that I must place a bit of emphasis on this point. Some persons get sick and wonder why the pastor does not call on them. My fellow Christian, it is your responsibility, if you are able, to send for the elders of the church. In preaching we are commissioned to go into all the world to every creature (Mark 16:15), but in healing we are to await the call of the sick. Unless you have notified your church officially and requested someone to visit you, there is no room for complaint on your part. Brethren, there are several benefits to be derived from your sending for the elders when you are sick. It would relieve the loneliness and longing of your own heart, erase any false conceptions on the part of your loved ones, and save some painful regrets on the part of the elders. Remember now, the first step in healing is to be taken by the sick, not the elders. If you feel it the duty of the elders to visit the sick, it is here stated that it is the duty of the sick to call for the elders.

The question arises next as to who the "elders" are. In Acts 14:23 we are told that the elders were those who were appointed in the local churches. When "they" (the Apostles Paul and Barnabas) "appointed for them" (A.S.V.) (the converts in any given locality) elders, they commended them to the Lord. The Greek word translated "appointed" is *cheirotoneo,* which means to stretch out the hand, suggesting that the Apostles stretched out the hand to indicate a person to thus appoint him. I am merely pointing out here that I can find nothing in the Scripture to indicate that the elders were elected by the people. The idea of voting is not indicated in the New Testament Church.

An elder will show himself to be such by his life. "And the Lord said unto Moses, Gather unto Me seventy men of the elders of Israel, whom thou knowest to be the elders of the people, and officers over them; and bring them unto the tabernacle of the congregation, that they may stand there with thee" (Num. 11:16). Moses did not make these men elders, but they had already shown by their lives that they were elders. Only the Holy Spirit can make a man an elder (Acts 20:28). The saints in any local assembly should get to know the overseers (1 Thess. 5:12, 13), and respect and support them, "especially they who

labour in the word and doctrine [or teaching]" (1 Tim. 5:17).
Peter and the other Apostles were teaching elders (see 1 Peter
5:12), and they apparently worked closely with those elders
whom they appointed (Acts 15:2, 4, 6, 22, 23; 16:4).

The appointed elder was literally *an aged person,* not a very
old person in the strictest sense of the word, but a believer who
had had the experience of walking with the Lord in prayer and
the study of the Word. A man may qualify to be an elder in position who is not an elder in age, and conversely, not all men who
are elders in age qualify to be elders in position. If I understand
the context of 1 Timothy 5 correctly, the Apostle Paul is instructing Timothy, the pastor-in-chief and overseer, how he
should choose and appoint elders or underseers. All sorts of problems are arising constantly in local assemblies, and these can be
faced and ruled over only by men with a sound head and heart.
Such men must be "blameless, the husband of one wife, having
faithful children not accused of riot or unruly . . . not self-
willed, not soon angry, not given to wine, no striker, not given to
filthy lucre; But a lover of hospitality, a lover of good men,
sober, just, holy, temperate; Holding fast the faithful word as he
hath been taught, that he may be able by sound doctrine both to
exhort and to convince the gainsayers" (Titus 1:6-9). Timothy
adds, "Apt to teach" (1 Tim. 3:2). "And the servant of the Lord
must not strive; but be gentle unto all men, apt to teach, patient" (2 Tim. 2:24).

Here, then, is the type person the sick are to call for. In the
local assembly, such as we have here in Bristol, it is always well
for the sick to make known their request directly to, or through,
the pastor or the one who has been set over you in the Lord
(Heb. 13:7, 17). He, in turn, will take the matter before the
other elders for prayer and consultation. On the other hand, if
the request should come directly to an elder other than the
pastor, the same procedure of prayer and consultation with the
pastor and board of elders should be carried out.

Now that the first major step has been considered, namely, the sick calling for the elders of the church, look at the next step. *"Let them pray over him. . . ."* You have no doubt noticed the importance of prayer throughout this Epistle. It has been stated that James was given the nickname of "camel's knees" because his knees were as hard as camel's knees, the reason being obvious —he was a man of prayer. (See 1:5-7; 4:2, 3, 8; 5:13-18.) In 5:13 we are exhorted to pray when any emotional experience comes to us. Here in 5:14 the elders are to pray for the sick. After all, what more sensible and practical thing than to pray could we do for the sick? We can bring them to no better place than the Throne of Grace.

Let it be clearly understood that the elders have no healing powers. As far as healing is concerned, elders are no different from other saints. The healing power rests alone with Him to whom they pray. Being the spiritual leaders in the domestic life of the local congregation, the elders are to be men of prayer. Any local church is blessed when praying men are on the official board —not that the faith is to be placed in the elders but rather in the Lord. The custom of praying for one, or a group praying together, showed that they were standing together in dependence upon God. When God used Elisha in the raising of the Shunammite's son, we are told that Elisha "prayed unto the Lord" (2 Kings 4:33). God answered his servant's prayer, but certainly no one could give the credit to Elisha for the miracle performed. It is worthy of note here that even our Lord, before raising Lazarus from the dead, "lifted up His eyes, and said, Father, I thank Thee that Thou hast heard Me" (John 11:41). Whatever else we are to learn from this statement in James 5:14, we must not over-look the importance of prayer when sickness comes to the children of God.

Returning to our text once again we note that after praying over the sick, the elders are told to anoint "him with oil in the name of the Lord." In treating this matter of anointing, I am constrained to remind my readers that the claim of the Roman Catholic Church that this passage gives the Romanist priest a warrant for practicing the "sacrament of extreme unction" has no foundation whatever. One need not be a theologian to see the Roman fallacy. The alleged purpose of "extreme unction" is to prepare a soul for death, while the purpose of anointing in this passage is to restore a sick person to health and preserve life. Roman apologists make it their practice to seize upon the most unlikely passages to support their unscriptural dogma.

In order that our readers see clearly that this is the common practice of the Roman Church, the following quotation is taken from the book *The Faith of Our Fathers* by James Cardinal Gibbons. "Extreme Unction is a Sacrament in which the sick, by the anointing with holy oil and the prayers of the Priests, receive spiritual succor and even corporal strength when such is conducive to their salvation. This unction is called *Extreme,* because it is usually the last of the holy unctions administered by the Church.

"The Apostle St. James clearly refers to this Sacrament and points out its efficacy in the following words: 'Is any man sick among you; let him bring in the Priests of the Church, and let them pray over him, anointing him with oil in the name of the Lord, and the prayer of faith shall save the sick man; and the Lord shall raise him up; and if he be in sins, they shall be forgiven him.' " By no stretch of the imagination could one honestly arrive at such an interpretation of James 5:14, 15.

Examine more closely the use of oil in our text. Are we to assume from James 5:14 that the use of means for healing is wrong? Are we to refuse the use of physicians, dentists, optometrists, and hospital facilities? Paul had as one of his companions in the gospel, Luke, "the beloved Physician" (Col. 4:14; 2 Tim. 4:11; Philemon 24). Then, too, our Lord said: "They that be whole need not a physician, but they that are sick" (Matt. 9:12). Of course He was answering the question of the Pharisees as to why He ate with publicans and sinners; but He certainly would not have used the physician, who was known to all, had He not been sympathetic toward his profession. Christ, the Great Physician of souls, came primarily to heal sinners of the soul disease of sin, but He sanctioned the work of the medical doctor too. Every sinner needs the Saviour; the man sick in body may need a physician. Our Lord always has been concerned with both the spiritual and physical needs of mankind, and it is not for any of us to limit whatever means He may be pleased to use.

Are we to assume that the healing power is in the "oil" with which the sick one is anointed? I do not believe that the oil was in itself a healing ointment. The anointing with oil was doubtless an external one, for certainly there is no cure-all known to man; that is, an oil that could be taken internally to cure any type of disease. David said: "Thou anointest my head with oil" (Psalm 23:5). "It is like the precious ointment upon the head, that ran down upon the beard, even Aaron's beard: that went down to the skirts of his garments" (Psalm 133:2). Actually the "oil" in James 5:14 would be no different from the muddy waters of the River Jordan into which Naaman was commanded to dip seven times. Naaman was healed of his leprosy in response to his faith and obedience, not because there was any healing power in the waters of Jordan (2 Kings 5:1-14). True, we are told in James to anoint the sick with oil, but the point here is not oil or no oil, but believing prayer or no believing prayer. If oil were not available, you may be assured that, without the oil, *"the prayer of faith shall save the sick."* But we must bear in mind that God has been healing people miraculously, and He continues to do so, in unique ways, sometimes without both oil or elders.

Let the elders proceed according to James, but let there be no room for the pastor or evangelist traveling about with a bottle of oil in his pocket, anointing those for whom he prays.

"And the prayer of faith [not the anointing with oil] *shall save the sick, and the Lord shall raise him up."* Now when healing is sought after, according to James, it is the elders who are to pray over the sick. This is an important observation since modern "faith healers" usually attribute failures of the sick to get well to the sick person himself. If there is any failure, then it

rests with those who pray; but according to James, there can be no failure when the divine order is followed. If we are going to accuse anyone of lack of faith, let us not accuse the sick person. Let those who officiate examine their hearts in the matter. Divine healing does not come through faithless praying. When the elders are agreed that God has given them the faith to believe Him for the healing of the sick person, then let them proceed according to the Word and God will perform the miracle. "Therefore I say unto you, What things soever ye desire, when ye pray, believe that ye receive them, and ye shall have them" (Mark 11:24). Not everyone who calls for the elders, who is anointed with oil, and who is prayed over, is healed; but when God gives the prayer of faith to the elders, "the Lord *shall* raise him up." The context leaves no doubt that healing will be effected when the conditions are met. The elders can say as did Peter to Aeneas: "Jesus Christ maketh thee whole" (Acts 9:34).

It seems to me that such cases of healing as here described in James would not be numerous. Not even the Apostles themselves could heal all the sick in whom they were interested. Paul, for some reason, could not pray the prayer of faith for Trophimus, for he left his friend at Miletum sick (2 Tim. 4:20). The case of Trophimus, and even of Paul himself (2 Cor. 12:7-9), prove that bodily healing is not always in God's will. Before the elders ask God for healing, let them be certain they are praying according to His will. Good and godly people died in apostolic times and will continue to die in our time. We must seek the mind of the Spirit of God, and in so doing we will undoubtedly discover that He might forbid us to offer the prayer of faith just as He forbade Paul to preach the Word of God in Asia. Just remember, if it is always the Lord's will to heal the sick, those for whom we pray would never die.

Consider one thought more in verse fifteen: ". . . and if he have committed sins, they shall be forgiven him." At once we can see here the possibility of the sick man being in this condition as a chastisement for sin. That God chastens with sickness because of sin is seen throughout the Bible. Some specific sins resulting in God's sending disease to the body have been: jealousy (Num. 12:1-10), rebellion (Num. 16), discontentment (Num. 21), adultery (Num. 25 cf. 1 Cor. 10:8), and partaking of the Lord's Table in an unworthy manner (1 Cor. 11:30). Quite often, although not always, sin and sickness are related (Matt. 9:2; John 5:14). Some Christians I have known have been frank to admit that sin brought on their sickness. The lesson in our verse is clear. Let us search our hearts first when sickness comes to us before ever we seek healing for our bodies. Confession and repentance of sins is obviously a necessary requisite to bodily healing. Oh, how much the elders need to know the mind of the Holy Spirit in the matter of praying for healing lest they unwittingly anoint one and pray for one who has been living in sin! It is not a case of dealing with the sin question generally but with sins specifically. Now not all who have been healed of disease have confessed and forsaken all known sin, but genuine repentance and confession are presupposed here before the healing, according to James, can be effected. After all, the sin question is the most important one, and we can rest assured that He who forgives all our iniquities can heal all our diseases.

"Confess your faults one to another, and pray one for another, that ye may be healed. The effectual fervent prayer of a righteous man availeth much" (5:16). I take it that this verse is a part of the Apostle's discussion on bodily healing. His words, "that ye may be healed," tell us that he is still speaking to the "sick among you." Some hold the application of "healed" to be wider than merely deliverance from bodily disease. Maybe so, but we know for certain that at least bodily healing is in the context.

Verse 15 concludes with the words, "And if he have committed sins, they shall be forgiven him," thereby suggesting the possibility of the sick person having committed some sin. The possibility becomes a probability in verse 16, for here it is clearly stated that there can be no healing until there has been confession. Whatever the faults or blunders or sins are, they must be confessed before the prayer of faith can operate. "If I regard iniquity in my heart, the Lord will not hear me" (Psalm 66:18) is a divinely written law of prayer. It is utter foolishness for one to look to God for miraculous healing if there is sin in the life that has not been confessed. "He that covereth his sins shall not prosper: but whoso confesseth and forsaketh them shall have mercy" (Prov. 28:13).

Quite often physical health and spiritual health are closely related. This is not always so, however, for such was Gaius who was sound in spiritual health but obviously weak physically (3 John 2). Here it is clearly illustrated that not every case of physical infirmity denotes spiritual weakness. On the other hand, the Christian who, when sick, seeks divine healing according to this Scripture, must of necessity confess all known sin. Now every believer should confess his sins daily to God, for "If we confess our sins, He is faithful and just to forgive us our sins, and to cleanse us from all unrighteousness" (1 John 1:9). However, we are told here to confess our faults to one another.

This confession of faults to one another does *not* mean what the Roman Catholic Church teaches it to mean. Romanism makes James 5:16 the ground for their confessional, whereby Roman Catholics must tell their sins to some Roman priest. Here in James we must recognize that a mutual confession is enjoined: "Confess your faults one to another." H. A. Ironside relates how a Roman priest pointed to this Scripture when insisting that it taught confession to one of his order. His hearer responded, "I will confess my sins to you if you will confess yours to me." Of course, the priest refused to recognize the mutual confession that James teaches. Again I am constrained to remind my reader that the Roman Church uses most unlikely passages of Scripture to support its beliefs.

Who are to confess their faults one to another? I see no change of persons from those mentioned in verse 14, namely, "the sick" and "the elders of the church." I know of no principle of Biblical interpretation that will warrant the interpreter to read into the context a change that is not there. The sick want healing, and the elders of the church are present to pray for the healing. Since no one else is included in the context, it follows that the sick and the elders of the church are to confess their faults one to another. After all unconfessed sin has been confessed, those who have gathered for the healing are to "pray one for another." Please make special note of the fact that they are to tell no one but God about the sins of their brothers or sisters in Christ. James 5:16 does not mean that the members of any local assembly are to stand up and publicly confess their sins. I am not stating disapproval of the public confession of sin where necessary. No doubt there are certain sins that seriously affect the whole assembly of believers; such demand public confession that all may know these sins are not tolerated among God's children. But most of our sins are between God and ourselves, and to scatter these abroad among gossipers and busybodies, as well as those who are spiritual, does much damage to the testimony of our Lord Jesus Christ.

Perhaps this is the place to add a word concerning the importance of confessing our faults to those whom we have wronged. Here is a lost art in our day. Rarely do we hear of one Christian going to another to confess his wrong in some quarrel or estrangement. "Therefore if thou bring thy gift to the altar, and there rememberest that thy brother hath ought against thee; Leave there thy gift before the altar, and go thy way; first be reconciled to thy brother, and then come and offer thy gift" (Matt. 5:23, 24). Until this is done we are utterly unfit for worship. Whether you have really offended your brother or sister in Christ, or if he or she wrongly feels that you have, go at once and see that the matter is straightened out. No religious performance is acceptable to God if there is uncharitableness, envy, ill-feeling, and the like.

"The effectual fervent prayer of a righteous man availeth much." James is saying here that the supplication of a righteous man produces much in results. Some Christians miss altogether the experience of direct answers to prayer. Others have periodic

experiences of closeness to God when, under the pressure of some
great trial of affliction, they get down to a life of real prayer.
James is not speaking of the mere saying of formal prayers, no
matter how fervently one may recite them, but he has in mind
the earnest supplication of a godly man for some specific need.
In our text the need is bodily healing.

Effectual prayers are prayers that effect results. There is nothing more clearly taught in Scripture than that prayer is a divinely
ordered means of God's children obtaining blessing. Some years
ago a well-known and able preacher came to our local assembly
to minister the Word of God for one service. He announced as
his subject "The Sense and Nonsense of Prayer." "The nonsense
of prayer," he said, "is the foolish idea in many Christians' minds
that prayer changes things." He said: "Prayer changes nothing,
nor does prayer change any person." I had to disagree. I have
seen prayer change situations and people. The Bible says there is
a kind of praying which is "effectual": that is, praying which is
powerful enough to produce the desired or intended effect. I am
not saying that prayer changes the plans and purposes of God but
surely we will not disagree with our Lord, who said: "Ask, and it
shall be given you; seek, and ye shall find; knock, and it shall be
opened unto you" (Matt. 7:7), nor with James who wrote by
inspiration, saying: "Ye have not, because ye ask not" (4:2).
God answered the prayers of men like Abraham, Moses, David,
Joshua, Elijah, Daniel, Paul, and a host of others, and be certain that He still answers the effectual, fervent prayer of a righteous man.

In further pursuit of the meaning of James here on the subject
of divine healing, do not overlook the important fact that the
elders, if they expect to see results, must be "righteous" men. We
assume now that these elders are saved men, so that their position
in Christ takes them out of the category of the "none righteous"
(Rom. 3:10); but positional righteousness is not all that is
meant by James. Let the elders who go to pray for the healing
of the sick be righteous in word and deed—not in position only

but in practice as well. If the elders are not holy men of God, they need not look for results; for "The eyes of the Lord are upon the righteous, and His ears are open unto their cry" (Psalm 34:15).

James now uses a classic illustration in Scripture to encourage the kind of praying that produces the intended effect. "Elias was a man subject to like passions as we are, and he prayed earnestly that it might not rain; and it rained not on the earth by the space of three years and six months. And he prayed again, and the heaven gave rain, and the earth brought forth her fruit" (5:17, 18). We are to learn first from these verses that the holy prophets who wrought miracles through prayer are members of our frail family, men with a nature exactly like our own, but men who dared to take God at His Word. The Elias (Elijah) who believed God for the miracle of which James writes and which is recorded in 1 Kings 18 is the same man who, in the very next chapter (1 Kings 19), fled in fear from the woman Jezebel. The kind of praying we are discussing here does not need to wait for perfect men, else no man, save Jesus Christ, ever could have prayed thus. It can be the praying of any one of us, even as it was of Hezekiah who prayed back his forfeited life (2 Kings 20:1-7), or Elijah on Mount Carmel. In spite of his weakness, Elijah yielded his life to God and wrought mightily through prayer. So may we!

Oh, worship the King,
All glorious above!
Oh, gratefully sing
His power and His love;
Our shield and defender,
The Ancient of Days,
Pavilioned in splendour,
And girded with praise.

Thy bountiful care,
What tongue can recite?
It breathes in the air,
It shines in the light;
It streams from the hills,
It descends to the plain,
And sweetly distils in
The dew and the rain.

Frail children of dust,
And feeble as frail—
In Thee do we trust,
Nor find Thee to fail:
Thy mercies, how tender,
How firm to the end!
Our Maker, Defender,
Redeemer and Friend!

O measureless Might!
Ineffable Love!
While angels delight
To hymn Thee above,
The humbler creation,
Though feeble their lays,
With true adoration
Shall sing to Thy praise.

CONCLUSION

James 5:19, 20

19. Brethren, if any of you do err from the truth, and one convert him;
20. Let him know, that he which converteth the sinner from the error of his way shall save a soul from death, and shall hide a multitude of sins.

The sinning one here, as in verses 15 and 16, is a believer, any of the "brethren." This is an excellent conclusion to the Epistle, for throughout, James has been attempting to turn erring saints back to the Lord. To convert means to "turn again." How easy it is at times to err from the truth both doctrinally and morally! The world, the flesh, and the devil, all three militate constantly against the truth of God. Negligence in prayer, Bible reading, assembling with other believers, witnessing for our Lord as He gives us opportunity, and a host of other things, all tend to lead the child of God away from the truth.

Now when we know that one of our brethren has departed from the truth, doctrinally or practically, a solemn responsibility rests with us. We are to attempt to get him to "turn back," that is to "convert" him. The word "convert" here is not synonymous with "save" or "regenerate." It is sometimes used of believers, as our Lord used it when speaking to Peter. He said to His erring disciple: "I have prayed for thee, that thy faith fail not: and when thou art *converted*, strengthen thy brethren" (Luke 22:32).

Yes, I am my brother's keeper (Gen. 4:9). "Brethren, if a man be overtaken in a fault, ye which are spiritual, restore such an one in the spirit of meekness; considering thyself, lest thou also be tempted" (Gal. 6:1). And James is speaking to "brethren" about "brethren." He is not speaking about witnessing to the unsaved, but rather of turning back the sinning saint. In 4:8 he says to believers: "Cleanse your hands, ye sinners." The church needs a ministry to the sinning saints. I long to see those who are walking with God learn how to restore those in the faith who have fallen. It is a Scriptural practice totally foreign to many Christians today.

But it is a fruitful ministry. When we are able, through prayer and personal work, to turn back a sinning saint from the error of his way, we "save a soul from death." This expression, "save a soul from death," does not refer here to the unsaved. It applies to the "brethren," to "any of you." The word "soul" here is better rendered "life." It is not spiritual death that James is writing about since no believer in Christ can die spiritually. Believers have passed out of death into life (John 5:24); they have been "quickened" (made alive) (Eph. 2:1). Our Lord said: "Whosoever liveth and believeth in Me shall never die" (John 11:26). Our Apostle is speaking of physical death since "there is a sin unto death" (1 John 5:16) for Christians. Paul speaks of the sin unto death for Christians in 1 Corinthians 11:30.

Our Lord used the word "soul" in speaking of a man's life. He said: "For what shall it profit a man, if he shall gain the whole world, and lose his own soul?" (Mark 8:36). Luke, recording this statement by Christ, writes, "For what is a man advantaged, if he gain the whole world, and lose himself, or be cast away?" (Luke 9:25). Here we see that the soul is the self. When God created man from the dust of the earth, He breathed into man the breath of life, and man became a living soul (Gen. 2:7). We speak of man possessing a soul when actually the soul is the man. Thy Soul is thyself. Peter, writing by inspiration of the Holy Spirit, referring to Noah and the flood, says: "Eight souls were saved by water" (1 Peter 3:20). We use the same expression today if we want to say that eight lives were saved by water.

What a precious ministry this is! How privileged the child of God is when called upon to turn back an erring brother from sin!

The spiritual brother may be sparing the life of his erring brother for extended usefulness in the service of the Lord.

When the sinning one is led to confess his sins to God, all of his sins are covered, and "Blessed is he whose transgression is forgiven, whose sin is covered" (Psalm 32:1). Many a Christian has been removed from this earth far sooner than he would otherwise have been because there was no one to lead him to turn back.

Do not tell me this is no business of yours. It most certainly is your responsibility and mine. We need the tenderness of James for our brothers and sisters in Christ who have gone astray. Such passion will not permit us to gossip about them nor turn from them, but will contrariwise draw us to them in loving concern. Biblical Christianity has a message of divine love for the unsaved, but no stronger appeal will be made to those who are outside of Christ than to see Christians loving and restoring their own who have fallen. This is indeed the Spirit of our Lord Jesus Christ.

BIBLIOGRAPHY

Bible Knowledge (All-Bible Graded Series of Sunday School Lessons), Vol. II (James). Chicago: Scripture Press, 1954.

BROWN, CHARLES. *The General Epistle of James.* London: The Religious Tract Society, 1907.

CALVIN, JOHN. *Calvin's Complete Bible Commentaries—Catholic Epistles.* Complete, unabridged translation by Henry Beveridge. Grand Rapids, Mich.: Wm. B. Eerdmans Publishing Co., 1948.

ERDMAN, CHARLES R. *The General Epistles.*

IRONSIDE, H. A. *Notes on James and Peter.* New York: Loizeaux Brothers, Inc., 1947.

JOHNSTONE, ROBERT. *The Epistle of James.* Grand Rapids, Mich.: Baker Book House, 1954.

KING, GUY H. *A Belief That Behaves.* London: Marshall, Morgan & Scott, Ltd., 1941, 1942, 1945, 1951.

LUCK, G. COLEMAN. *James.* Chicago: Moody Press.

NEIGHBOUR, R. E. *The General Epistle of James.* Cleveland: Union Gospel Press.

NIEBOER, JAMES J. *Practical Exposition of the Epistle of James.* Erie, Penna.: Our Daily Walk Publishers, 1950.

PLUMPTRE, EDWARD HAYES, ed. *The Epistle of St. James* (Cambridge Bible for Schools and Colleges). New York: Cambridge University Press, 1895.

ROSS, ALEXANDER, ed. *Commentary on the Epistles of James and John.* Grand Rapids, Mich.: Wm. B. Eerdmans Publishing Co., 1954.

SEUME, RICHARD. *Studies in James.* Paterson, N.J.: Madison Avenue Baptist Church.

SIMPSON, A. B. *"Christ in the Bible" Series—James.* Harrisburg, Penna.: Christian Publications.

SPENCE, H. D. M., and EXELL, JOSEPH S., eds. *Pulpit Commentary —Hebrews and James* (v.21). New York: Funk & Wagnalls Co., 1895.

INDEX OF SCRIPTURE TEXTS

INDEX

Abraham, 112-116, 184, 201, 222
  justified, 113-116, 195-196
Aeneas, 218
Affliction
  definition, 206
  fruits, 11
Ananias, 170
Anointing, 215-217

Belshazzar, 189

Chastening, 11
Christians, two natures, 134-135,
  151-152
Confession, 219-221
Conversion, 226-227
Covetousness, 183

Daniel, 196, 222
David, 126, 217
Deity of Christ, 7
Disobedience, 95

Elders, 213-215, 217-218, 221, 223
Elijah, 13, 222-223
Elisha, 215

Faith, 13
  fruits of, 4, 69-70, 77, 105-106
  in prayer, 24, 217
  justification, 3
  living, 117
  rewarded, 42
  saving, 51, 108-110, 113
  test of, 65
  trial of, 13-14
Flesh, 37, 135, 151-152

Gaius, 220
Gethsemane, 208

Gomorrah, 189
Grace of God
  leveling effect, 28-29
  privileges, 158

Healers, 211-212, 217-218
Heart, 36
Hezekiah, 206
Holy Spirit, 4, 15, 134
Humility, 166-167

Isaiah, 124-125
Israelism, British, 8

Jehovah's Witnesses, 7
Jeremiah, 196
Jerusalem, 184
Jews, 112-113
  brethren in Christ, 10
  scattering, 7-8
Jezebel, 13, 223
Job, 124, 162, 184, 197
John, 137
Jonah, 207
Jordan River, 217
Joseph, 197
Joseph of Arimathæa, 184
Joshua, 201-202, 222
Jude, 4
Judgment, 82-83, 99-101, 171-172,
  184, 186, 187, 196
Justification, 3
  cause and effect, 115
  through Christ, 115

Labor, 186-188, 192
Liberality (God's), 43-44
Luther, 3, 4

Manasseh, 206

241